MW01599203

Construction Zone

FriendZone • FamilyZone • FaithZone

PrēTeen ELECTIVES AGES 10-12

A Curriculum for Preteens

STANDARD PUBLISHING
Cincinnati, Ohio

Construction Zone

268.43
SEN

Westlink Church of Christ

About the Authors

Patricia A. Senseman has been an editor at Standard Publishing for seven years. Formerly a Director of Children's Ministries, she is a popular speaker at conventions and seminars. She has contributed to several books, including *Great Worship for Kids.* Most importantly, Patricia and her husband, Mark, teach Ben, Laura, Aaron, and their fourth grade friends every Sunday morning.

Robin S. Hooper has been a teacher at the elementary level and is currently a school librarian in a Columbus, Ohio, Christian elementary school. She has co-written material for Standard's Vacation Bible School curriculum. Robin works with elementary through high school ages in Sunday school, VBS, camp, Sunday evening programs, and Bible Bowl.

Barbara J. Tolly is a preschool teacher in Columbus. She has worked with preteens in Sunday school, Vacation Bible School, and Sunday night programs at church and camps.

Kristi Walter has been writing and editing Bible-based material for elementary kids for twelve years. Kristi has taught almost all of the lessons she's written or edited. She's taught elementary kids in Sunday school, youth group, and church camp. Kristi also teaches writing at Crosswalk Christian School in Sublette, Kansas.

Cover design and illustration by Ryoichi Yotsumoto
Inside illustrations by Ryoichi Yotsumoto/Sandy Wimmer

All Scripture quotations, unless otherwise indicated, are taken from the HOLY BIBLE NEW INTERNATIONAL VERSION®, NIV®. Copyright ©1973, 1978, 1984 by International Bible Society. Used by permission of Zondervan Publishing House. All rights reserved.

The Standard Publishing Company, Cincinnati, Ohio
A Division of Standex International Corporation
©1996 The Standard Publishing Company
All rights reserved
Printed in the United States of America

03 02 01 00 99 98 97 96   5 4 3 2 1
ISBN 0-7847-0501-1

Construction Zone

Beyond childhood, heading to the next level, preteens live in a hard-hat construction zone. Help them build positive friendships, reinforce family ties, and form lasting church relationships. Help them learn the secrets to winning in real life!

0904-2187

Why "Next Level"?

Upper elementary kids—we'll call them preteens—are reaching, striving, groping toward the next level. They're in transition. They want to be taller, stronger, faster, and smarter as they catapult on their way to the next level.

In some ways preteens appear already to have arrived at the next level (once termed junior high). Preteens want to wear the right clothes, match hairstyles with athletes or rock stars, and fit in with the peer group no matter what! For many, however, the next level is an elusive goal: manly muscles and feminine curves are controlled by hormones not purchasing power.

So, too, the limits on thought structure. Many, if not most, fifth and sixth graders lack the ability to think critically, form logical arguments, or draw general principles from specific examples. There is usually a wide gulf between their level of experience and their ability to reflect on the meaning of their experiences.

Preteens are also still resolving the issue: *What can I do well?* rather than tackling the adolescent question: *Who am I?* So when preteens dress and act like their peers, they are striving for self-acceptance—feeling that they are as up-to-date as their peers, rather than endeavoring to establish a personal identity. Erickson's studies show that ten to twelve year olds are less involved with establishing a personal identity than they are with figuring out what they're really good at. This disparity creates difficulties for those using junior high curriculum for preteen classes: "What you see (a teenager) is not what you get (concrete-operational thinking and a different life task)."

Next Level curriculum is transitional: to help transitional preteens feel comfortable in teen-style learning settings and to equip leaders to teach within the limits of a preteen's limited development. Sessions are structured to help you teach preteens effectively in groups. The younger the student, the more discussion guidance must be given to identify appropriate conclusions and to suggest appropriate actions to be taken.

While many junior high topics are helpful and many elective curriculums look age appropriate, they often do not work with preteens because they were not designed for their limited thought processing and inexperienced discussion skills.

Next Level Preteen Electives! Planned and designed with preteen issues in mind and tailored for the learning capabilities of concrete thinkers! Visually appealing for the video generation. Emotionally satisfying for techno-driven kids.

This curriculum offers bonus opportunities for preteens to **Go to Extremes** serving others. It also strives to build family relationships—**Bridge the Gap**—during fun-filled family sessions.

So, because life is not a game—
pick a topic and recruit some helpers.
Start a group for ten to twelve year olds—
They'll be glad you did!

Next Level Preteen Electives address the importance of instilling values for character development.

This curriculum includes positive, choice-making strategies, friendship-making skills, care-giving and service skills, as well as refusal strategies (when appropriate). Each preteen in the program should feel accepted, important, and supported!

Surveys of Christian educators, Sunday school teachers, and Christian parents encourage us not to abandon the teaching of fundamentals. That's why Next Level curriculum includes units designed to equip kids to use the Bible, offers a survey of Bible heroes, and help kids fit in at church, among other topics. Future books will build mission awareness, encourage a strong sense of biblical stewardship, and help kids reconnect with adults who will guide them to maturity.

You can use Next Level Preteen Electives confidently, knowing that it is based on core biblical principles, permeated with Bible teaching, and presented in a way that ten to twelve year olds can understand and enjoy!

How are Next Level units organized?

Get Into the Game

As an introduction to the session, this large-muscle activity grabs the students' attention and encourages participation from the entire group.

Step 1

This section provides three activities that may be set up as learning centers or used as options. Depending on the class size, the teacher may divide the class into three groups. Each works on an activity. For this to be effective, ample assistance is needed.

If the class is small, the teacher can customize the session to fit that need. Select one or two options to utilize or have the class work together instead of dividing into small groups.

Each activity is designed to help students dig deeper into the topic. A biblical study is always included in this section.

Step 2

This section is designed as a presentation time. Each group reports on its findings from Step 1. Again, if the teacher customizes the first step for the entire class to work on together, presentations can be made immediately following the activities in Step 1.

Step 3

This activity involves the entire class in one group. This will help students apply what was learned in Steps 1 and 2.

Take It to the Next Level

This final section concludes the session by helping students commit the principles they have learned to their own lives. The question, "So what does this mean to me personally?" can be answered in this section.

Extra Helps

Each unit introduction includes devotion suggestions for either the teacher and/or the students. The devotional ideas correlate with the sessions contained in that particular unit.

Reproducible pages are provided for your convenience. Photocopy these pages for your personal use or for your students' use to enhance each session.

Additional Resources

The following list of books, games, magazines, and music serve as extra resources for each unit. Choose from these materials as research prior to teaching or as extra activities.

Unit 1—FriendZone

The Friendship Connection by Timothy Jones, Tyndale House Publishers, Inc.

A House Full of Friends (How to Like the Ones You Love) by Susan Alexander Yates, Focus on the Family Publishing

Life Stories Board Game

The Ungame for Kids

Best Friends fiction series (girls) by Crossway Books

"Friends" by Michael W. Smith (Reunion Records)

"A Friend Like U" by Geoff Moore and the Distance (ForeFront Communications)

Unit 2—FamilyZone

15 Minute Family Traditions & Memories by Emilie Barnes, Harvest House Publishers

Children at Risk by Dr. James Dobson & Gary L. Bauer, Word Publishing

Family Shock: Keeping Families Strong in the Midst of Earth-shaking Change by Gary R. Collins, Tyndale House Publishers, Inc.

Let's Make a Memory by Gloria Gaither & Shirley Dobson, Word Publishing

"First Family" by Rich Mullins (Reunion Records)

"Talk It Out" by D.C. Talk (ForeFront)

Unit 3—FaithZone

I Caught a Little, Big Fish: Fishing for Faith in the Heart of Your Child by Jill Briscoe & Judy Golz, Vine Books (Servant Publications)

103 Questions Children Ask About Right From Wrong by David R. Veerman, James C. Galvin, James C. Wilhoit, Daryl J. Lucas, Richard Osborne, and Lil Crump, Tyndale House Publishers, Inc.

101 Questions Children Ask About God and *102 Questions Children Ask About the Bible* by James C. Wilhoit, David R. Veerman, Richard Osborne, James C. Galvin, and Daryl J. Lucas, Tyndale House Publishers, Inc.

"That Kind of Love" by PFR (Sparrow)

"Facts Are Facts" by Steven Curtis Chapman (Sparrow)

Unit 1

Friendship Under Construction

Your preteen students know how important friendships are. They may not know, however, the way to go about making and keeping a friend. These sessions will help your students understand how to make and keep friendships. But more importantly, these sessions will help your students understand how to make and keep friendships based on godly principles. Each preteen will begin to become a godly friend.

How do you talk with preteens about constructing friendships? One of the most important things to remember is openness. Admit when you have struggled with a friendship. Talk genuinely about a time you lost a friend.

Try not to minimize the difficulty students experience with friends. Though the problems may not seem so major to you, remember that you are not that age anymore. Friendship difficulties are very real and painful to them.

Listen intently to what students say. As they talk about their intimate interactions with others, you will have a window to their hearts.

Above all else, model the characteristics of godly friendship. Practice forgiveness, kindness, patience, and compassion in your classroom.

Session 1
Know the world's rules and God's guidelines for being a friend.
Feel convicted to become a godly friend.
Work on being the kind of friend God says is good.

Session 2
Know the characteristics of a godly friend.
Feel convicted to become a godly friend.
Begin to choose friends based on God's guidelines.

Session 3
Know the nurturing qualities of a godly friendship.
Feel convicted to become a godly friend.
Commit to nurturing godly friendships

Session 4
Know a godly plan to combat trouble in friendships.
Feel convicted to become a godly friend.
Commit to being a godly friend even when it is difficult.

Unit Projects

Interviews

Guide your students to interview a pair of friends. They can talk with a parent, an elderly neighbor, a classmate, or a sibling. Friends can be any age. Your students will benefit in learning about friendships between people of all ages. Encourage students to come up with a list of questions to ask. Here are a few to get them started.

How did you meet each other?

What do you like to do together?

What advice would you give for making friends?

What do you like best about your friend?

What do you like least?

Do you ever disagree? How do you work it out?

Bring a Friend

Invite your own friend to come to one of the class sessions. The two of you can talk about your friendship—how it started, what you have experienced together, why you are friends. Your students will enjoy getting to know your friend and seeing you interact.

Dear Frieda Friend Advice Column

Set up a station in your classroom where students can write a note to Frieda Friend asking for advice on being a friend. Purchase an inexpensive mailbox for the students to put their letters in. Frieda could answer their notes at the end of each class session. Frieda can be a character that an actress plays or she could answer the students' letters in writing for you to read.

Friendship Building Games

Any group games that will work at building cooperation and interaction among your students are appropriate for these sessions. How exciting it would be to see friendships develop in your class because of this study!

Daily Devotions

To build yourself into a godly friend, you need to know several things.

First, you need to know what a godly friend is. You find that out from God by reading His Word, the Bible. Studying God's Word will help you begin to become a godly friend.

Second, work on being a godly friend every day. Each day read the Scripture reference listed. Think about what it tells you about being the kind of friend God wants you to be.

Week 1	Week 2	Week 3	Week 4
Characteristics of a Godly Friend	**Jesus Is a Godly Friend**	**The Proverbs Friend**	**Jesus Tells About Being a Friend**
Read what the Bible says a godly friend is.	Read Bible examples. Jesus shows us how to be a friend.	Read Proverbs. See what Solomon says about being a friend.	Read what Jesus says about being a godly friend.
Monday 1 Corinthians 13:4-7	**Monday** John 8:3-11	**Monday** Proverbs 1:10, 11, 15, 16, 18	**Monday** The Good Samaritan Luke 10:25-37
Tuesday Ecclesiastes 4:9, 10, 12	**Tuesday** John 4:4-30, 39-42	**Tuesday** Proverbs 4:14; 10:12; 11:12	**Tuesday** The Light of the World Matthew 5:14-16
Wednesday John 15:13-15	**Wednesday** Luke 18:15-17	**Wednesday** Proverbs 13:10, 20; 15:1, 18	**Wednesday** Love and Forgive Matthew 5:38-44
Thursday Philippians 2:3	**Thursday** John 14:2, 3	**Thursday** Proverbs 16:7; 17:9, 17	**Thursday** The Sinful Woman John 8:1-11
Friday Ephesians 4:26, 27, 29	**Friday** Luke 22:15-20	**Friday** Proverbs 24:1; 27:6, 17	**Friday** Love Your Enemies Luke 6:27-31

Paving the Way for Godly Friendships

Scripture. 1 Corinthians 13:4-7;
Ecclesiastes 4:9, 10; John 15:13-15;
Proverbs 17:17; Romans 5:8;
Philippians 2:3

Know the world's rules and God's guidelines for being a friend.
Feel convicted to become a godly friend.
Work on being the kind of friend God
says is good.

Get Into the Game

Randomly divide students into two groups. Appoint one group
to prepare an argument for the statement, "God does care who
my friends are." Appoint the other group to prepare an argument for the opposite statement, "God does not care who my
friends are." Instruct students that whether they agree or disagree with the statement, they must take the assigned viewpoint in the debate. Give students approximately five
minutes to prepare their statements.

Group 1 will have two minutes to present their argument,
"God does care who my friends are." Use a stopwatch or
kitchen timer to monitor the two minutes. Group 2 will then
have two minutes to present their argument, "God does not
care who our friends are." Group 1 will follow with a one-
minute rebuttal for its position. Group 2 will then have one
minute to give its rebuttal.

State that, as you work together through these sessions
about making and keeping friends, the students will develop a
greater understanding of what God teaches about the friends
they choose.

Step 1

Activity 1—"Good Day USA" Broadcast

Students will write and produce an episode of "Good Day
USA" The show can be recorded with a video camcorder
and shown later in the group session. One group of three to
four students will be the production crew—organizing the
segments and providing the hosts for the show. The rest of
the students will work in pairs—learning about two biblical

Materials
Bibles, index cards, miscellaneous props,
camcorder, poster board, marker

11

friends, and then acting as those characters in the broadcast. Specific directions for the groups follow.

Production crew. Designate one member to be Joan Louden and one, Charlie Gilbert, the show's hosts. They will interview the pairs of friends. The other crew member(s) can be a cameraman or a prompter, holding a cue card with the interviewer's questions. Make the cue card using the poster board and marker. This group needs to develop questions to ask the pairs of friends, such as: "How did you meet?" "Why are you friends?" "How do you know he cares about you?" "What is special about your friendship?"

Pairs of friends. These students will research a pair of biblical friends and be prepared to answer an interviewer's questions on the "Good Day USA" show. Assign each pair a group of Scriptures to read and answer these questions. The questions can be written on the index cards.

Why are they friends?

How did they show their love for their friend?

What characteristics can you learn from their friendship?

David's friend, Jonathan—1 Samuel 18:1-4; 19:1-6; 20:4; 23:15-18

Lazarus's friend, Jesus—John 11:1-7, 11-14, 32-44

Paul's friend, Barnabas—Acts 9:19-21, 26-28; 11:25, 26; 15:37-40; 2 Timothy 1:2-8

Timothy's friend, Paul—Acts 16:1-5; 1 Corinthians 4:17; Philippians 2:19-23; 2 Timothy 1:2-8

Each student may want to use a prop for his particular character. Here are some suggestions:

David—musical instrument, shepherd's staff (large umbrella with a curved handle)

Jonathan—robe to give to David

Lazarus—grave clothes (strips of cloth)

Paul—suitcase, handcuffs

Barnabas—suitcase

Timothy—large envelope addressed to Timothy with Paul's return address

A brief summary of the friends' relationships follows to help you draw out some of the important facts.

Jonathan loved David as himself. Jonathan gave David his robe, tunic, and armor as a sign of their friendship. Jonathan protected David when Saul wanted to kill him. Jonathan encouraged David when he was afraid Saul would kill him.

Jesus visited Lazarus and his sisters, Mary and Martha, often. They lived just outside Jerusalem in Bethany. Jesus cried when

He knew Lazarus was dead. Jesus raised Lazarus from the dead.

Barnabas told people about Paul so they would know that he did not want to harm them. They worked together in the church. Paul and Barnabas disagreed about Mark traveling with them. Paul later realized that Barnabas was right about Mark.

Paul and Timothy shared similar interests. The growth of the church was important to them. They worked and traveled together. Paul loved Timothy; he prayed for him; he missed him. Paul encouraged Timothy as a Christian.

Suggested discussion questions: Which of the Bible friends is your friend most like? Why? Which of the Bible friends do you want to be like? Why? What would you need to change to be like one of these Bible friends?

Activity 2—What Is a Friend?

Students will brainstorm characteristics of a friend. Instead of using the typical brainstorming technique, however, use a process called story boarding.

Give each students a stack of 15-20 index cards. You will state a category. The students will think of as many "thoughts" that relate to the topic as they can in sixty seconds. Instead of the students shouting out their "thoughts" and your writing them on a chalkboard or piece of paper, the students will write their own thoughts on the index cards. As each student writes on an index card, he calls out his "thought" aloud. He then tosses the index card in the center of the table. Another "thought" is written on another index card and so on until the sixty seconds has elapsed.

Students will write on index cards at the same time. One "thought" is written per index card. Allow sixty seconds for each category. Do not be concerned about duplicate thoughts until you are sorting the cards later.

Once the students have had an opportunity to story board the categories, it is time to sort the index cards. Use these titles as headings:

Friend   **Nonfriend**

Tape all of the index cards on a wall one by one under these two headings. Discard any duplicates. Sorting into only two categories will challenge your students to be definitive about where the qualities fall. Then sort the cards under "friend" into two more categories:

God   **Other**

Suggested discussion questions: What qualities do you admire most in a friend? What quality is your strongest with

Materials
index cards, kitchen timer or wrist watch with a second hand, drafter's or painter's masking tape, pencils or pens

Categories
Qualities of a friend
Qualities of an enemy
Qualities of a friendship that failed
Qualities of your mom's or dad's friend
Qualities of Jesus as your friend

your friend? your weakest? What quality from the nonfriend list do you struggle with?

Optional Affirmation Activity

Pin a large index card on the back of every student. Students can walk around and write on the index cards a quality of a friend that they admire in that person. Be sure to participate yourself.

Students can then look at what their classmates wrote about them. Encourage your students to save the index card and read it again when they are discouraged or feel hurt.

Activity 3—Scripture Study

Students will summarize what they learn about being a friend from the Scripture references they read. Guide students to look up and read the Scripture references. Then, they will place the characteristics of a godly friend in the acrostic F-R-I-E-N-D.

1 Corinthians 13:4-7—Love is directed outward toward others and not inward toward ourselves. Being a godly friend has many facets of giving without expecting anything in return.

Ecclesiastes 4:9, 10—Life is designed for companionship not isolation. Friendship improves our lives and makes us healthy.

John 15:13-15—Jesus' love for us on the cross shows that He is our friend. We, too, should show sacrificial love.

Proverbs 17:17—Loyalty is one of the greatest evidences of a genuine friendship. A godly friend is there for his friend even when it is difficult.

Romans 5:8—Godly friends can love as God loves; He loved us before we loved Him.

Philippians 2:3—Godly friends are humble, treating others with respect and courtesy.

Encourage each student to choose one verse to memorize that has significant meaning to him as a friend. Students can make tags using a paper clip and large adhesive labels.

Write the verse on the tag and draw a design on two adhesive labels. Stick the labels together with the paper clip in between. The tag will look like a ski lift tag or the tags that often come on novelty bags. Students can put the tag on the zipper pull of their jackets, purses, backpacks, or sports bags.

Materials
photocopies of page 17, Bibles, pencils or pens, large paper clips, large adhesive labels

Step 2

Present the "Good Day USA" show. Following the presentation of the broadcast, discuss friendship in general with your students. Tie in examples from the Bible relationships.

Jonathan's friendship with David was so important to him that he was willing to stand up to his own father, King Saul, in order to defend David. Jonathan and David had a covenant relationship—their friendship was more important than any other earthly relationship. Marriages are covenant relationships in today's society. They were willing to die for each other.

Jesus loved Lazarus and his sisters, Mary and Martha. When Lazarus died, Jesus was very sad and even wept when He saw how sad Mary, Martha, and the mourners were.

Paul and Barnabas show us that friends can and will disagree. They probably decided that they would agree to disagree about Mark traveling for the cause of Christ. Even though they traveled separately for a while, Paul and Barnabas remained friends.

In Paul and Timothy's friendship, we see how friends encourage each other. Paul taught Timothy and was older than Timothy, yet they were good friends. We know that even when Paul and Timothy could not be together, Paul prayed for his friend.

Suggested discussion questions: What characteristics of a good friend do you see in Jonathan? Jesus? Barnabas? Paul? Which Bible person do you want to be most like in your friendships? Why (and be specific)? What would you need to work on to be more like that Bible person?

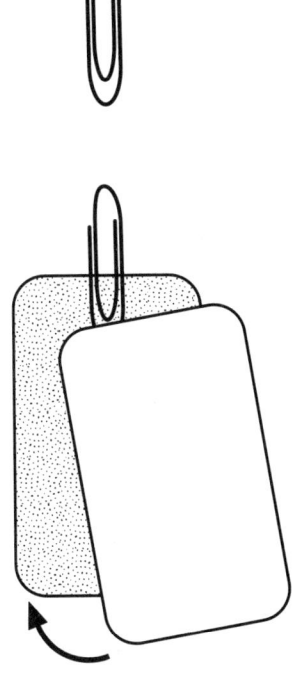

Step 3

Guide students to make a list of God's guidelines and the world's views on a sheet of poster board. Include the qualities from the Bible friends, the story board list, and the Scripture references on the reproducible page.

Place the poster board in the room turned in such a way that each student can approach and view the list one at a time. It could be placed on an easel or taped to the side of a cabinet.

Give each student a different colored marker. Guide the students to go to the poster one by one. Each student will circle the qualities, no matter whether they fall under God's guidelines or the world's views, that best describes who she is as a friend. When all the students have had a chance to mark their qualities, have a student tally the results. Discuss with your students the top three qualities they circled in the God's guidelines category. Affirm the ways your students are making and keeping friends according to God's guidelines.

Save the poster board so you can read and study it later. You will learn a lot about the makeup of the group of students you will be teaching. By looking at the qualities your students circled, you will be able to project what to emphasize in the next few sessions.

Instruct students to make a friendship bracelet for themselves as a reminder that they can make godly friendships based on the principles they have discovered and discussed.

A friend loves at all times, and a brother is born for adversity.

Proverbs 17:17

Using two strands of three bright colors of embroidery floss, students will braid the thread to make a bracelet. Tie the six strands in a looped knot about four inches from the end. Braid the three colors together to within four inches of the other end of the strands and make a knot. The braided portion of the embroidery floss should be about the circumference of the student's wrist or ankle, depending on where he plans to wear it. The knots on either end can be covered with one or two of the strands of embroidery floss simply by wrapping it around the other strands and tying it off. (Note: students have probably made similar bracelets and may have their own way of weaving one. Encourage them to do so. The important element of this friendship bracelet is that it appears to have three basic sections.)

As the students work on their bracelets, discuss Ecclesiastes 4:12: "Though one may be overpowered, two can defend themselves. A cord of three strands is not quickly broken." As your students make friends based on God's guidelines, they are inviting God to be involved in their friendships. He can be the third strand between two friends.

Take It to the Next Level

Ask students to take the quiz to see what kind of friends they are.

Close the session with a prayer circle, thanking God for the friendships we have and asking Him to make us the kind of friends He would want us to be.

Quiz

1. If you asked one of my friends what kind of friend I am, he would say,
   A. "He's a godly friend."
   B. "We aren't friends."
   C. "He's a wanna-be godly friend."

2. I am most like this Bible friend:
   A. Jonathan
   B. Jesus
   C. Barnabas
   D. Paul
   E. None of the above
   F. All of the above

3. Of the following characteristics, this one is the easiest for me:
   A. Loyal
   B. Considerate
   C. Loving
   D. Giving

4. Of the following characteristics, this one is the most difficult for me:
   A. Loyal
   B. Considerate
   C. Loving
   D. Giving

5. Which of these best describes your interest in being a godly friend?
   A. "I can't wait to learn more about it."
   B. "I know all I need to know about being a friend."
   C. "I'm just here for the food."
   D. "It probably won't help me to have friends since I don't have any now."

What Is a Godly Friend?

Read these Scripture passages about being a godly friend. Think of a characteristic of a godly friend from the Scripture that begins with each letter in "friend." Write it in the acrostic puzzle.

1 Corinthians 13:4-7
Ecclesiastes 4:9, 10
John 15:13-15
Proverbs 17:17
Romans 5:8
Philippians 2:3

 ©1996 by The Standard Publishing Company. Permission is granted to reproduce this page for ministry purposes only—not for resale.

Building a Friendship

Scripture. Luke 10:25-37, 18:15-17; John 4:4-30, 39-42; 14:2, 3; 15:12, 13

Know the characteristics of a godly friend.
Feel convicted to become a godly friend.
Begin to choose friends based on God's guidelines.

Get Into the Game

Before class, inflate two balloons with helium. With a permanent marker, write "agree" on one balloon and "disagree" on the other. Tie each to a stationary object on opposite sides of the room.

Instruct students that you will make a series of statements. Each student is to decide individually if he agrees or disagrees with a statement. The students who agree with a statement will move to stand under the "agree" balloon. The students who disagree with a statement will cross the room and stand under the "disagree" balloon.

Then discuss why the students agree or disagree with a statement. Accept any reason for agreeing or disagreeing. Encourage all of the students to participate. You may want to ask a specific student a question about a statement to solicit participation. Students may express a belief that you or other students disagree with or is contrary to God's guidelines for friendship. That is OK for now. This activity is to get the students talking about friends. You will find out what they really believe.

Here are some suggested statements. Add some of your own that you think are applicable to your group. Use popular song lyrics about friends and relationships that your students will be familiar with.

- Friendships just happen.
- Having one best friend is better than having many friends.
- Christians are supposed to be friends with everyone.
- You can be friends with someone the same sex as you.
- God created us to be independent and depend *only* on Him.
- To have a friend, be a friend.
- Friends are friends forever.
- Being a friend is more give than take.

Materials
two balloons, helium, permanent marker, string

18

Step 1

Activity 1—Alphabet Game

Write each letter of the alphabet on two sets of 26 lima beans. Place both sets of lettered beans in the bowl. Instruct students to draw a 12-box grid on their paper.

One by one, students take a bean from the bowl. Each student writes one characteristic of friendship that begins with the letter on the bean in a box on his grid. The students continue to draw beans until their grids are full with twelve characteristics of a friend.

Now play an alphabet game. One student randomly chooses an alphabet bean from the bowl and announces the letter. The first student to say a characteristic from her grid that begins with that letter receives the bean to put on her grid. Once a student has a bean on a square, he cannot state that characteristic again. The student to get five beans in his grid boxes wins.

Suggested discussion questions: Of all the characteristics of a friend we listed, which one describes a trait you possess? one of your friends? Which characteristic describes Jesus? Tell about a specific way Jesus demonstrated that characteristic?

Activity 2—"Jesus Is a Godly Friend" Scripture Study

Using the reproducible page, guide students to look up the Scripture references. Each reference recounts a time Jesus was demonstrating a characteristic of a godly friend. Instruct students to identify that characteristic and write about it on the appropriate blank.

Students can then list some other characteristics of a godly friend Jesus possessed.

Here is a summary of the passages.

John 8:3-11—A woman who had committed adultery was brought to Jesus. Jesus said, "If any one of you is without sin, let him be the first to throw a stone at her" (John 8:7). In this event we see Jesus being compassionate and forgiving of sin. We can learn about judging others. Jesus did not condone what the woman had done but told her to stop sinning. It is God who judges sin, not us. A godly friend shows compassion and forgiveness.

John 4:4-30, 39-42—Jesus told the Samaritan woman about the living water He had to offer as the Messiah. Even though this woman was a Samaritan and Jesus was a Jew, He still talked to her. Samaritans were hated by Jews. The Samaritan woman's sins were well-known: she had several husbands and was living with a man who was not her husband. The woman did not value the same truths that Jesus valued, yet He chose to spend some time with her in order for her to understand

Materials

a bag of lima beans, a felt-tipped permanent marker, paper, small bowl

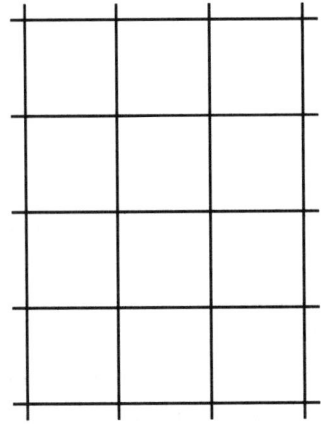

Materials

Bibles, photocopies of page 25, pens or pencils

who He was. Jesus witnessed to the Samaritan woman. A godly friend tells about Jesus at every opportunity.

John 15:12, 13—We are to love as Jesus loved us. He loved us so much that He died for us. We may not be called to die for a friend, but we can give sacrificial love. A godly friend loves unconditionally by listening, encouraging, and spending time with a friend.

Luke 18:15-17—Jesus had time for the children because they had the kind of faith we should have. Even though the disciples thought the children were unimportant, Jesus made the time with the children a special time for them. A godly friend spends time with friends who may be unimportant to others.

John 14:2, 3—Jesus teaches about going to prepare a place for us, and returning to get us and take us to that place. He is talking about eternity. Jesus can be trusted. What He says He will do. A godly friend is reliable and trustworthy.

Suggested discussion questions: Which characteristic of Jesus is the easiest for you as a friend? The most difficult? Which characteristic do you want to develop in yourself? How do you plan to do that? How can you be compassionate and forgiving? tell a friend the gospel? love unconditionally? spend time with someone who is unimportant to others? be reliable and trustworthy?

Activity 3—Good Samaritan Scripture Study

The students will develop a modern-day drama using the parable of the good Samaritan from Luke 10:25-37. Guide students first to read and discuss the Scripture passage. They will identify people today that are like each character in the parable. Use the following information as a help in guiding the conversation.

• The law expert was a scholar who wanted to discuss the man who was robbed and left to die. Examples today: news anchor, sociologist.

• The robbers were the perpetrators who wanted to harm the man. Examples today: abusive family member, bully.

• The priest and Levite might have been curious about the wounded man but wanted to avoid the problem or did not want to get involved with him. Examples today—This could be anyone who ignores someone who is in pain: parent, teacher, peer.

• The Samaritan saw the injured man as a person to befriend, to care for, to love. This is the example of a godly friend you want to hold up as a standard for your students to adopt.

• Even though the innkeeper took care of the man, the injured man was merely a customer in his business establishment.

After studying and discussing the Scripture, guide students to develop and rehearse a drama. The situation they use for their

Materials
Bibles, note paper, pens or pencils, miscellaneous props: a necktie, an apron, a ball cap, a large school jacket, straw hat, athletic equipment, backpack

drama should have each person from the parable depicted in a modern-day character.

The students can improvise with the miscellaneous props you provide.

Suggested discussion questions: In your life, who are like the robbers? How do they make you feel? How can you respond to them? In your life, who are like the religious men? How do they make you feel? How can you respond to them? When do you have an opportunity to be like the Samaritan?

Optional Affirmation Activity

Ask everyone to sit in a circle on the floor. Limit the circle size to five or six people. Begin by reminding your students that this is a positive, uplifting, encouraging time. Instruct students to name a fruit or vegetable that would describe each person in the circle. They should be ready to explain why they chose that piece of fruit or vegetable for that person. Give everyone one minute to think about it and make their decisions. You may want to provide pens and paper for students to write down their choices.

Then go around the circle, choose one person, and have everyone tell what fruit or vegetable they chose for that person and why. Move from person to person one by one.

Step 2

Present the modern-day parable of the good Samaritan. Following the presentation, discuss characteristics of a godly friend. Include qualities of the Samaritan, Jesus, and the positive characteristics from the alphabet game in your discussion.

The Samaritan had grown up as an outcast. Samaritans were a mixed race of Jews and foreigners. He probably knew what it meant to be ignored, made fun of, and mistreated. Yet he was a godly friend. He showed love to a man he did not know. He could have cleaned and bandaged the injured man's wounds and then gone on down the road. But he even took him to a safe place and made sure he would be cared for.

Jesus showed compassion and forgiveness when the adulterous woman was brought to Him. He also showed love and acceptance as He talked to the Samaritan woman about living water. Jesus took valuable time to spend with the children whom others thought were unimportant. Jesus is a reliable friend because He not only loved us to the point of dying for us, but he has gone to prepare a place for us and will return to take us to be with Him. We know that He will do what He says.

Some of the characteristics of a friend (probably discovered in the alphabet game activity) are listed here for you to include in discussing qualities of a godly friend.

sense of humor	listens
cooperative	forgiving
reliable	keeps secrets
consistent	helpful
authentic	cares about feelings
unselfish	affectionate
kind	willing
accepting	understanding
encouraging	patient

Suggested discussion questions: When do you have an opportunity to be like the Samaritan? When you think of Jesus as your friend, what characteristic of a godly friend do you think of?

Step 3

Activity #1—Twister

Guide your students in playing a modified version of the game Twister. You can use an actual Twister game board or make your own by drawing and coloring 8-inch circles on a large piece of butcher paper. On each circle write one of these categories: Injured Man, Robber, Priest or Levite, Samaritan.

You will read the following descriptions and the students will place a hand or foot on the circle that matches the description. Two to four students can play on the same game board at one time. Other students will enjoy watching. Or use several game boards at the same time.

You may need to remind your students that the "Injured Man" is one who is in need of a friend; the "Robber" is one who causes pain; the "Priest or Levite" is one who ignores or avoids the injured man; and the "Samaritan" is one who is a friend of God.

Read a description from a category and allow time for students to decide what category the person fits in, move his hand or foot, and explain why he thinks that is the category. Then read a description from the next category and allow the students to respond. Continue until all of the descriptions have been read. The student still in position without having fallen over when all the situations have been read is the winner.

"Injured Man"

• "I don't think anyone at school really likes me. I wonder if it's because no one else in my class is really like me. Sure, there are girls, and there are girls with long hair, and there are kids who play the piano. But no one else is Asian."

Materials
Twister game board or 8-inch colored circles, butcher paper, markers

- "I could really use some help with math. We've started doing some pre-algebra in my class, and I just don't get it. I asked my brother and my dad, but they don't have time. John sits next to me in class. Maybe he'll help me during our study time."

"Robber"

- "Jan is so weird. Her hair is dyed shoe-polish black; she wears all black; even her nail polish is black. Her clothes are way too big and she's been talking about getting her nose pierced. Gross! I told her how weird she was yesterday at school. She just turned around and walked off."

- "I know I'm her dad but she just drives me crazy sometimes. She won't listen to me. She doesn't do what I tell her to and when I tell her to. I'm under so much pressure at work that I can't handle her when I come home. She is really asking for it when I hit her. She just isn't listening."

"Priest or Levite"

- "I know those jokes must hurt Jamie's feelings. But I'm too shy to stand up to everyone else when they are telling them. Greg is more bold than I am. Maybe he will say something about how rude the jokes are the next time."

- "I saw Chris crying at school today. It is probably about her mom and dad. I heard that they were getting a divorce. Living with just one parent is really tough. I should know. I hope she finds a friend that she can talk to."

"Samaritan"

- "Mike confided in me and told me all about the night he . . . . Oh, I can't tell you. Anyway, it is really hard to keep his secret but I told him I would. He trusted me not to tell."

- "I think she just needed to say it aloud. Once we talked about it, Amanda didn't seem as upset about her grade. I think I'll send her a note this afternoon to cheer her up."

Activity #2—Macaroni Reminder

Instruct students to read Proverbs 18:24. Work on memorizing the verse; then discuss what it means.

We all need friends who care about us, who will listen and be concerned about our needs. We all need friends who are reliable, who will stick by us through good times and bad times. It is a very special friend who will be your friend when it is tough. It is better to have one such friend than to have a lot of people that you call your friends, but who are not there when you need them.

What kind of friend are you? Are you a tough friend? Do you stick close to your friend when it is tough?

Guide students to glue the macaroni alphabet to the tongue depressor to spell out "Stick closer." Then instruct them to

Materials
macaroni alphabet letters, tongue depressors, glue, markers, magnets (optional)

color the alphabet with markers. The tongue depressor can be put any place that the student will see it frequently and remember to develop the characteristics of a godly friend. He may want to place it in the tumbler in the bathroom beside his toothbrush. She may want to stick it in a plant in her room. He may glue a magnet on the back and put it in his locker.

Take It to the Next Level

Instruct students to write a letter to God or to themselves.

Some students may feel very comfortable writing a letter to God as a prayer. Those students who wish, may feel more confident in writing a letter to themselves.

Whether the letter is to God or to self, the letter should express a willingness to become a godly friend. Two simple examples follow. Guide your students to write what they feel about being a godly friend.

Materials
paper or stationary, pens or pencils

> Dear God,
>
> I want to become a friend like Jesus was. I want to be more loving and forgiving. I want to reach out to people who may not be popular or important. Please help me try to be the kind of friend you would like for me to be. Thanks, and I love you.
>
> > Love,
> > Linda

> Dear Pat,
>
> I'm really proud of you sometimes. You try to be nice to people that are different or don't have any friends. You also let your friends know that you are a Christian.
>
> You could work on being more forgiving though. Don't forget that it is God's job to judge, not yours. Why don't you start with forgiving Bethany for losing your favorite jacket.
>
> I'm glad to see that you are making progress in being a godly friend.
>
> > Sincerely,
> > Pat

Close the session with prayer.

Jesus Is a Godly Friend

Read the Scripture passages. Write about the characteristic of a godly friend Jesus showed.

John 8:3-11

John 4:4-30, 39-42

John 15:12, 13

Luke 18:15-17

John 14:2, 3

Describe another time when you remember that Jesus showed that He was a friend.

 ©1996 by The Standard Publishing Company. Permission is granted to reproduce this page for ministry purposes only—not for resale.

Traveling a Bumpy Friendship Road

Scripture. Proverbs 1:10, 11, 15, 16, 18; 4:14; 13:20; 24:1; Romans 12:1

Know the nurturing qualities of a godly friendship.
Feel convicted to become a godly friend.
Commit to nurturing godly friendships.

Get Into the Game

Before class mark five areas in the room with a number one, two, three, four, or five. When the students have arrived, ask each student to stand by the number that is most appropriate for the way he would respond to the question or statement. Read the following statements one at a time. This activity will force the students to think about where they fall specifically on the "being a godly friend" continuum.

- On a scale of one to five, I'm a _____ at making friends.
- On a scale of one to five, I'm a _____ at keeping friends.
- On a scale of one to five, I'm a _____ at making godly friends.
- On a scale of one to five, I'm a _____ at giving in to pressure from friends when I know what they are doing is wrong.
- On a scale of one to five, I'm a _____ at talking to my friends about my relationship with God.
- On a scale of one to five, I'm a _____ at fighting with friends.
- On a scale of one to five, I'm a _____ at forgiving friends.

Materials
paper, marker, tape

Step 1

Activity 1—Top Ten

Students will make a poster with a list of the top ten ways to lose a friend. The students will see in the negative examples ways to nurture a friendship and prevent it from ending.

Instruct students to come up with ten statements of ways to lose a friend. A few of the statements can be funny or outlandish. Guide the students to order the statements from #10 to #1 in David Letterman style.

Materials
note paper, pens or pencils, used magazines, scissors, poster board

Then guide students to find type in magazines for the numbers on their poster. They can hand letter the statements. They may want to add photographs and art from the magazines to the poster as time allows.

Suggested discussion questions: Have you ever lost a friend? How did it happen? Was there something you could have done to save the friendship? What would be your top three list of things to do to save a friendship?

Activity 2—Friendship Case Studies

The students will read the case studies and develop questions about the friendships that will be discussed later in the lesson time. Guide students to think about what the positive characteristics are in the friendships of Tara and Jessica, and Brent and Jake. Then look at the negative characteristics. Guide them to write questions about what the problems may be, why there is tension, and what can be done about it. The questions should be thought questions, not easily answered by yes or no. In order to write good questions, the students will have to process some of the problems in the circumstances. Let them take their time, and give them some freedom in the discussion.

Case Study #1

Tara and Jessica were best friends in fifth grade. They did everything together. They didn't always have the same classes, but when they did, they tried to sit beside each other. They came home from school together. When they weren't at each other's homes, they talked on the phone. They could talk with each other about anything, even really personal stuff. Through the summer, they stayed in touch, too. Tara went to Jessica's house more because Jessica's mom was at home during the day.

Jessica even talked to Tara about going to church with her. Tara seemed interested, but when Tara asked her mom, she said no. Tara's family didn't go to church because her dad said that there was no God. Jessica and Tara talked about it one time, and Tara said she wasn't sure what she believed. She said she thought it was really hard to believe in someone you can't see. Jessica tried to talk to her about God one other time, but Tara changed the subject.

Now that sixth grade has started, Jessica and Tara are going to a new school. They don't have very many classes together. They see each other in the halls some. They ate lunch together at the beginning of the year but now they aren't doing that.

Tara seems to have some new friends. Jessica thinks her new friends are kind of wild. She's not sure why Tara is hanging around with them.

Jessica misses Tara and doesn't understand why they aren't such good friends anymore.

Materials
note paper, pens or pencils, photocopies of page 32

Case Study #2

Jake and Brent have been buddies since they were kids. They grew up around the corner from each other. They have always gone to the same school, played on some of the same ball teams, and been on the swim team together for three summers.

Brent and Jake were out in the ball field after school one day pitching a softball around with some other guys. Jake said, "Hey, look what I've got!" as he pulled a bottle of whiskey out of his backpack. Brent was very shocked. He knew that Jake's dad was an alcoholic, and the boys had talked about the fact that they would never drink that much. They had also learned in school that once a person gets started drinking, sometimes it is very hard to quit.

The other guys gathered around Jake and said, "What kind is it?" "Where did you get it?" "All right! Let's try it." Brent wanted to try it even though he knew it was wrong and illegal. He didn't want the other guys to think that he was weird or too good. So he tried it. Brent knew he shouldn't have drunk any of that whiskey the minute he felt it burn in his throat.

Suggested discussion questions: Have you ever had a friend like Tara? Tell us about the friendship. Have you ever had a friend like Jake? Tell us about being his friend.

Optional Affirmation Activity

Guide students to make a chain of paper cutout guys and gals. Then instruct them to write the names of people who have been their friends in their lifetime. (Students who believe they do not have any friends now will be able to write names of several they have had over the years.) The students can decorate the cutout figure to look like that friend. Next, guide students to write why they are a friend with that person. This activity will help students see that they have had several friends over the years and why they make the kind of friends they do.

Materials
paper, scissors, markers or crayons

Activity 3—Light Study

The students will experiment with placing a lit candle under a bowl. They will find that the candle will not give off light, and it may be extinguished from the lack of oxygen.

Choose a student to light the votive candle in the holder. Place the bowl over it. Discuss what happens.

• A candle's purpose is to give off light and it cannot function properly under the bowl.

• The candle may go out under the bowl because it cannot get enough of what it needs—oxygen.

Take the bowl off of the candle. Talk about the difference it makes in how the candle functions.

Materials
votive candle, votive candle holder, large dark glass or aluminum bowl

Instruct your students to look up and read Matthew 5:14-16. Discuss the Scripture passage with the students. Focus the conversation on how they can be the light of Jesus to their friends.

Suggest discussion questions: How are you the "light of the world"? How do you hide your light? How do you "let your light shine before men"?

Step 2

Students who read the case studies and wrote discussion questions will guide the other students in conversation.

Lead the students to make the following conclusions about friendships.

Case Study #1: Tara and Jessica

It appears that Tara has developed other friendships that do not include Jessica. Maybe Tara is uncomfortable with Jessica because she believes in God and goes to church. Maybe Tara is embarrassed because her dad will not let her go to church with Jessica. It sounds as if Tara's new friends are different from Jessica. Maybe Tara has some new interests that she does not have in common with Jessica.

Case Study #2: Brent and Jake

Brent feels pressure to do what the other guys are going to do—drink the whiskey. He knows it's wrong; he knows it's illegal; he knows he should not drink it. But he does it anyway. He does not want the other guys to make fun of him or put pressure on him to drink. So he decides to follow along with them.

Once students have discussed and made some conclusions about the case studies, instruct them to read the following Scripture references and talk about how they relate to the case study. Some notes are given to assist you in the discussion.

Case Study #1

Proverbs 13:20 (Be careful about choosing friends because we pick up some of their characteristics and values. Jessica may become more like Tara, which could hurt her relationship with Jesus.)

Proverbs 24:1 (We must desire to be like Jesus Christ, not wicked men. Jessica's friendship with Tara may end because of how important it is to Jessica to go to church and make that a priority in her life.)

Case Study #2

Proverbs 1:10, 11, 15, 16, 18 (Some sin may look very attractive or make us feel like part of the crowd, but it is still wrong. Brent wanted the other boys to think he was cool. Brent knew drinking the whiskey was wrong, but he did it anyway.)

Proverbs 4:14 (Friends sometimes try to make us sin. Jake

and the other guys were really excited about trying the whiskey. They probably knew that it was wrong too.)

Romans 12:1 (God wants us to live for Him completely. Brent knew that drinking the alcohol with his friends was not living for God completely.)

Suggested discussion questions: What can Jessica do to be a godly friend? Why would it be OK for Jessica to let her friendship with Tara end? Why should she try to keep it? When have you had trouble knowing whether or not to keep a friend? What could Brent do to be a godly friend? What made it so hard for Brent to stand up to Jake and say no? When has it been hard for you to say no to a friend?

Step 3

The students who made a list of the top ten ways to lose a friend can present it now. Guide students to come up with the top five ways to save a friendship. Write their responses on the back of the poster board or on a chalkboard.

Suggested discussion questions: Why would it be important to save some friendships? When is it OK for you not to save a friendship?

Encourage your students that it is natural to lose friends and make new ones. God wants us to have friends. God also wants us to have godly friends that love Him. Sometimes friends we have made are not godly friends. It is OK for those friendships to end if they are friends that tempt us to sin. Keeping those friendships may be good so that we can show them what being a Christian is all about too.

Students who participated in the candle experiment can demonstrate it now. Guide them to read the Scripture passage, explain what it means, and tell how each of them can show the light of Jesus to their friends. They need to include what it means to be the "light of the world," how we hide our light, and how we "let our light shine before men."

Note: During the first two sessions on friends, the students worked with fictional situations they may find themselves in with their friends. This session the students will move to working on specific circumstances in their own friendships. This may take more time. Allow the students to have freedom to talk and to express their feelings of frustration, guilt, and hurt about losing and saving friendships. The difficulties they are having in their relationships with friends may seem very trivial or silly to you, but they are very real and painful to them.

Divide students into pairs (guys with guys and girls with girls). Give the pairs the following instructions.

"Think of a time when a friendship you had was in trouble.

Work with your partner to act out the situation. Talk with your partner about what you did and what happened. Decide if it is what a godly friend would have done. If not, decide what that would be. You will act out the situation and talk about it with the class. You have eight minutes."

You may need to give the students a couple of examples showing the kinds of situations you are talking about. The situations in the case studies offer good examples. Other examples: being tempted to do something wrong, talking about a relationship with God, positively influencing a friend to do right. Allow students eight minutes to talk about the situation and come up with the actions and dialogue. Give a one-minute warning when their time is about up.

Guide each pair to act out the situation and talk about what happened with the rest of the class.

Suggested discussion questions: Did you handle the situation as a godly friend would? What would a godly friend have done? How could you have been Jesus' light in that situation? What other type of situation have you been in with a friend that was difficult? Did you do what a godly friend would have done?

Take It to the Next Level

Guide students to make a light of the world votive candle holder. They can light the candle in their room at home. It will remind them to be Jesus' light to their friends. The students could light the candle at home when they are having a difficult time with a friend to remind them about being a godly friend. They could light the candle to celebrate a time they showed Jesus' light to a friend or when they did the right thing in a situation.

Students will cut tissue paper into odd shapes no larger than one-inch square. Use watered-down school glue sparingly to randomly glue the tissue shapes on the outside of the glass votive candle. It will look like stained glass. The edges of the tissue paper pieces should be right next to each other and can overlap a little. Allow the glue to dry to at least a tacky feel. Using a black or blue permanent marker, outline the tissue paper shapes. Set the votive candle holder aside to let it dry. Trim any paper that extends above the candle holder. Insert a votive candle or tea light candle.

Ask a student volunteer to close the session with prayer.

Materials
tissue paper, glue, glass votive candle holders, permanent markers (black or blue), votive or tea light candles

0904-2187

Friendship Case Studies

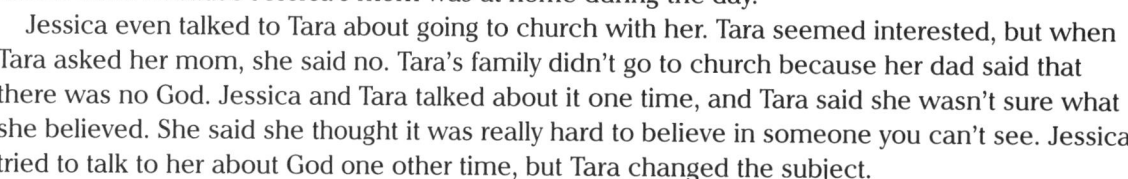

Case Study #1

Tara and Jessica were best friends in fifth grade. They did everything together. They didn't always have the same classes, but when they did, they tried to sit beside each other. They came home from school together. When they weren't at each other's homes, they talked on the phone. They could talk with each other about anything, even really personal stuff. Through the summer, they stayed in touch, too. Tara went to Jessica's house more because Jessica's mom was at home during the day.

Jessica even talked to Tara about going to church with her. Tara seemed interested, but when Tara asked her mom, she said no. Tara's family didn't go to church because her dad said that there was no God. Jessica and Tara talked about it one time, and Tara said she wasn't sure what she believed. She said she thought it was really hard to believe in someone you can't see. Jessica tried to talk to her about God one other time, but Tara changed the subject.

Now that sixth grade has started, Jessica and Tara are going to a new school. They don't have very many classes together. They see each other in the halls some. They ate lunch together at the beginning of the year but now they aren't doing that.

Tara seems to have some new friends. Jessica thinks her new friends are kind of wild. She's not sure why Tara is hanging around with them.

Jessica misses Tara and doesn't understand why they aren't such good friends anymore.

Case Study #2

Jake and Brent have been buddies since they were kids. They grew up around the corner from each other. They have always gone to the same school, played on some of the same ball teams, and been on the swim team together for three summers.

Brent and Jake were out in the ball field after school one day pitching a softball around with some other guys. Jake said, "Hey, look what I've got" as he pulled a bottle of whiskey out of his backpack. Brent was very shocked. He knew that Jake's dad was an alcoholic, and the boys had talked about the fact that they would never drink that much. They had also learned in school that once a person gets started drinking sometimes it is very hard to quit.

The other guys gathered around Jake and said, "What kind is it?" "Where did you get it?" "All right! Let's try it." Brent wanted to try it even though he knew it was wrong and illegal. He didn't want the other guys to think that he was weird or too good. So he tried it. Brent knew he shouldn't have drunk any of that whiskey the minute he felt it burn in his throat.

 ©1996 by The Standard Publishing Company. Permission is granted to reproduce this page for ministry purposes only—not for resale.

Session 4

Patching Potholes With a Friend

Scripture. Proverbs 10:12; 11:12; 13:10; 15:1, 18; 16:7; 17:9; 27:6, 17; Matthew 5:38-44; 18:15; Romans 12:17-21; Ephesians 4:26, 27, 29; Colossians 3:13; James 1:19

Know a godly plan to combat trouble in friendships.
Feel convicted to become a godly friend.
Commit to being a godly friend even when it is difficult.

Get Into the Game

Divide students into pairs. Put several three-foot masking tape lines on the floor around the room. Instruct the pairs that they will play a tug-of-war game. Give each pair a bath towel. Each player grabs one end and pulls. The player who can pull the other student across the masking tape line is the winner.

Discuss the similarities between playing the tug-of-war game and handling conflict in a friendship. When the player's partner was pulling on the towel and not giving in, it causes an adrenaline rush to resist. People can experience the same kind of adrenaline rush when conflict arises with another person. Either anger or competition can cause an adrenaline rush.

Suggested discussion questions: How did you feel when your partner was constantly pulling and you couldn't just let go of the towel? How are the feelings you had like the feelings you sometimes get when a friend does something you do not like?

Materials
masking tape, bath towels

Step 1

Activity 1—Common Conflicts

The students will think about times in their friendships that match the given conflicts. They will rehearse dialogue depicting that conflict. The mini-skits will be presented for the rest of the students to guess during Step 2.

Guide students to recall a time they have experienced conflicts in their friendships. They will then pick one of the situations, and with a partner, practice and present the situation for the other students to guess. Each mini-skit should last no longer than about thirty seconds.

Materials
index cards with situations written on them

33

Conflictive situations:

1. A friend ignores you.
2. A friend breaks something of yours that is important to you.
3. A friend is using you to get what he wants.
4. A friend is spending more time with another friend than she is with you.
5. A friend asks your advice or opinion and then does not listen.
6. A friend is critical of something you did, said, or wore.
7. A friend does not stick up for you when someone else is teasing you.
8. A friend does not forgive you for hurting his feelings.

Suggested discussion questions: How did you feel when you were in conflict with your friend? How do you think your friend felt? What did you do to resolve that situation with your friend? What else could you have done to resolve that conflict?

Activity 2—Scripture Study

The students will read Scripture references that talk about what to do in different types of conflictive situations. To help them more fully understand the verses, guide them to rewrite each verse in their own words.

Instruct the students to look up and read aloud the Scripture passage. Then look up and read the Scripture passage in several other versions of the Bible. If there are words they do not understand, they can look them up in the dictionary. If there are still phrases in the verse that they do not understand, guide them to discuss it with an adult teacher. The information about the verses below will be helpful if the students get stumped.

Proverbs 10:12—Hating someone only makes a bad situation worse. Loving someone makes it easier to forgive him when he does something wrong.

Proverbs 11:12—A godly friend will not say everything she thinks or feels at the time. She will wait until she has had time to think about it.

Proverbs 13:10—Pride will cause quarrels. A godly friend has a humble spirit that will accept advice and admit being wrong.

Proverbs 15:1—When friends argue it is with loud words that hurt the other person. When gentle words are used with a gentle voice, it is difficult to be angry.

Proverbs 15:18—A friend who gets angry quickly will make arguments worse. A friend who is calm and thinks through his anger will not have as many conflicts with his friends.

Proverbs 16:7—When we love God and are godly friends, even people who do not like us will not bother us.

Materials

Bibles, several versions and paraphrases of the Bible (*The Message* would be a good version for this activity), pens or pencils, a dictionary

Proverbs 17:9—A godly friend is willing to forgive his friend's sin against him. It is tempting to bring up old sins when arguing with a friend. That just makes the conflict worse.

Proverbs 27:6—A friend may have to tell a friend something tough but he knows it is for his own good. The friend knows his friend loves him and wants what is best for him. An enemy will say anything and may not be genuine about it.

Proverbs 27:17—Two friends who bring their ideas together can help each other become better people.

Matthew 5:38-44—When someone does something wrong to us, we want to get back at them. Jesus says that we should want to love and forgive them instead. Jesus also tells us to pray for the people who are mean to us.

Matthew 18:15—This verse gives Jesus' guideline for a godly friend to confront a godly friend. The friend should go talk to his friend instead of going away from his friend hurt or upset.

Romans 12:17-21—A godly friend will always be kind and forgiving. He will try to not have conflicts with his friends. He will be considerate even to his enemies.

Ephesians 4:26, 27, 29—A godly friend gets angry when it is appropriate. He does not let it build up inside. But he also does not lose his temper for every little reason. A godly friend also remembers that her words can be very harmful or encouraging. She is careful with everything she says.

Colossians 3:13—A godly friend knows how much God has forgiven him. He realizes that he must forgive his friend like God forgives him.

James 1:19—A godly friend listens carefully and speaks carefully. He does not get angry quickly when he has been wronged.

Suggested discussion questions: Which Scripture reference talks about something that you already do as a godly friend? Which Scripture reference talks about something you need to work on with your friendships?

Optional Affirmation Activity

Use an instant-type camera to take a snapshot of each of your students as they arrive in the classroom. Post the photo on a bulletin board you have prepared before class. The bulletin board should be brightly colored and have a heading that reads, "We are godly friends." During class, ask the students to list a characteristic that tells about that person beside his picture. The characteristics should come from the list in Galatians 5:22, 23 where the fruits of the Spirit are listed. A student can list as many characteristics beside a picture as she wishes. At the end of class, cut the bulletin board apart so that each student can take his picture and the list of characteristics home with him.

Materials
instant-type camera, film, bulletin board, paper, markers

Activity 3—Putting Out the Conflict Fire

Begin by showing a short excerpt from the video (less than one minute). Talk about the devastating effects of fire on a building. Discuss that most fires start from something very small, maybe just a spark, and grow slowly to a raging fire out of control. Talk about the horrible damage from fire and smoke, and from the water used to put fire out. Also talk about the fact that many fires can be prevented if people take the necessary precautions. Discuss what some of those precautions are.

Then have your students imagine that the last fight they had with a friend was a fire that got out of control. They will investigate the fire using the following questions.

Divide students into triads to talk about the last fight one of them had with a friend and to answer the questions on the reproducible page.

• What spark started the fire?
• What did I do to fuel the fire?
• When did the fire get out of control?
• What damage did the fire do?
• What could I have done to put out the fire?
• Did I act like a firefighter or an arsonist?
• If someone starts a fight near me again, how will I respond?

Suggested discuss questions: Would you say that you are a firefighter or an arsonist? Do you have the equipment you need to prevent fires in your friendships? What equipment do you have? What equipment do you still need? Do you think you have the necessary equipment to fight fire? What would your tools be?

Materials
a video recording of a fire (a recent newscast in your community, a home video, or a short segment from a movie such as Backdraft), television, VCR, photocopies of page 39

Step 2

Divide the group into pairs. Take one student from each pair outside the classroom. Instruct them that no matter what their partner says, he must disagree with him. He can be pleasant about it, but he must disagree. Tell the students you are going to ask several questions and you want them to give a different answer than what their partner says. Bring the students back into the classroom and assemble the pairs.

Tell the student pairs they will make some decisions about seeing a movie together. Ask the following questions and pause to give the students an opportunity to discuss their answers. One student in each pair will disagree with the other student.

1. What video would you like to see?
2. At whose house will you watch it?

3. Will you invite other people or will it be just the two of you?

4. What will you eat while you watch the movie?

Once you have asked the questions, ask the pairs what decisions they made. You will find they were not able to decide because one partner was disagreeable. Talk about how that made the other student feel. Talk about how the disagreeable student felt when he was creating conflict.

Let several students share about real situations with a friend when they felt some of those feelings.

Instruct students who prepared mini-skits about the conflictive situations to present them now. The other students will guess what situation the students are depicting. Write the situation on a piece of poster board or the chalkboard. When all of the students have presented their mini-skit, move on to matching the Scripture passages with the situations.

Students who studied and rewrote the Scripture passages can match the situations to any Scripture references that apply. More than one Scripture reference may apply to a situation. Guide students to read the Scripture passage from their Bibles and then read their rewritten paraphrase. Discuss what each Scripture passage means to the conflictive situation.

Suggested discussion questions: What are five things a godly friend would do when there is conflict in a friendship? How do you feel when there is conflict in a friendship? How do you think you would feel knowing you had something to do with getting rid of that conflict?

Step 3

Instruct the students to work in groups of three or four for this activity. Assign each group one of the conflictive situations discussed earlier. Tell them they will work together to make up another mini-skit that will present the response of a godly friend they discovered in the Scripture passages. Give the student groups five to six minutes to rework the mini-skit. Give them a one-minute warning when the time is up.

Allow each group of students to present their mini-skit for the rest of the class. The remainder of the students may have suggestions for other ways the conflict could be resolved. Discuss those other ways as each group presents their mini-skit.

When all of the groups have presented their mini-skits, instruct the students to come up with five actions to take when conflict arises in a friendship. The five actions should be based on the Scripture passages that have been studied during this session. The students could think about each action being on a finger of their hand. That may help them remember the actions when they are in conflict with a friend.

Here are some suggestions for the actions based on the Scripture passages that have been studied.

Proverbs 10:12—Love makes it easier to forgive.

Proverbs 11:12—Think about what you want to say.

Proverbs 13:10—Be humble not proud.

Proverbs 15:1—Use gentle words and a gentle voice.

Proverbs 15:18—Don't get angry quickly.

Proverbs 16:7—Love God.

Proverbs 17:9—Forgive your friend's sin against you.

Proverbs 27:6—Sometimes being a friend means being tough on a friend.

Matthew 5:38-44—Love, forgive, and pray.

Matthew 18:15—Go toward a friend when there is a conflict.

Romans 12:17-21—Be kind and forgiving.

Ephesians 4:26, 27, 29—Don't get angry when it is not appropriate. Don't let it build up inside. Remember that words can be harmful.

Colossians 3:13—Forgive friends like God forgives you.

James 1:19—Listen carefully and speak carefully. Don't get angry quickly.

Take It to the Next Level

Instruct students to take a second look at the analogy of a fire when dealing with conflict in a friendship. Students will work individually. Each student will think of a situation when they had a conflict with a friend. Then they will answer these questions listed on "Putting Out the Conflict Fire."

• What spark started the fire?

• What did I do to fuel the fire?

• When did the fire get out of control?

• What damage did the fire do?

• What could I have done to put out the fire?

• Did I act like a firefighter or an arsonist?

• If someone starts a fight near me again, how will I respond?

Encourage students to take the time right now to pray by themselves about being a godly friend who will work at putting out fires. The students could spread out all over the meeting area and spend about three minutes alone to pray and think about being a godly friend.

Close the session with prayer. Ask God to help you and your students continue to develop godly friendships.

Materials
photocopies of page 39, pens or pencils

Putting Out the Conflict Fire

Proverbs 10:12
Proverbs 11:12
Proverbs 13:10
Proverbs 15:1
Proverbs 15:18
Proverbs 16:7
Proverbs 17:9
Proverbs 27:6
Proverbs 27:17
Matthew 5:38-44
Matthew 18:15
Romans 12:17-21
Ephesians 4:26, 27, 29
Colossians 3:13
James 1:19

• What spark started the fire?

• What did I do to fuel the fire?

• When did the fire get out of control?

• What damage did the fire do?

• What could I have done to put out the fire?

• Did I act like a firefighter or an arsonist?

• If someone starts a fight near me again, how will I respond?

 ©1996 by The Standard Publishing Company. Permission is granted to reproduce this page for ministry purposes only—not for resale.

Bridge the Gap

"No Man Is an Island" Party

Plan a friend party for the entire family as the last session of this series of lessons. Your students will enjoy bringing their friends. And it gives the students' families an opportunity to celebrate friendships together.

Every family member is invited to come to the party and bring a friend. The party is designed so that family members of all ages will enjoy the time spent with their friends. Even preschool siblings can participate in the games. Adult parents and grandparents will have a good time with the relays and "The Friends Game," played in the style of "The Newlywed Game."

Students can make party invitations out of colorful paper and markers. Guide students to make an invitation for each family member. You may want to include an R.S.V.P. to help in your planning.

Each family member can bring a friend. The party needs to be planned so that the unchurched will feel comfortable attending with their friends. The party also needs to be inter-generational so that the entire family will have a good time.

Decorate for the party using an island theme. Make a big banner that says, "No man is an island. Celebrate friends." Use palm trees, sand, pineapples, parrots, and patio umbrellas to decorate. Purchase fun, colorful party supplies to use for serving the food.

Celebrate friends with the entire family.
- Explanation
- Make invitations
- Decorate the room
- Recipes
- Games

40

The students could prepare ahead of time a short presentation telling about each topic they have studied about being a friend. It could be as simple as a student talking about what he learned during a particular session. Or a group of students could present one of the activities they completed for a session.

Here are some ideas.

Session 1

• Students could present the "Good Day USA" show.

• Display the F-R-I-E-N-D acrostic poster on the wall during the party.

• One student could show and tell about her friendship bracelet. She could read Ecclesiastes 4:12.

Session 2

• A family group could play the alphabet game.

• Students could present their modern-day drama based on the good Samaritan parable.

• Students could recall characteristics of a godly friend.

Session 3

• Students could share their top ten list for losing friends.

• Students could perform the light experiment and show the votive candle holders they made. A student could read Matthew 5:14-16.

Session 4

• Students could read the Scripture paraphrases they wrote.

• Students could tell about how conflict in a relationship is like fire.

• Display the affirmation bulletin board.

Close with a short devotion. Read Ecclesiastes 4:9, 10. Talk about the importance of friends. Life is designed for companionship, not isolation. No man is an island.

Have a prayer circle with all of the friends holding hands. Thank God for the friendships that have been developed and ask for wisdom and guidance in making godly friends.

Serve snacks and drinks. The recipes included on page 42 could be prepared at the party by the friend pairs. Even the very young friends can help in some way. Use your imagination for the types of food to serve. You may want to have some snacks prepared in advance. Provide the ingredients for other snacks to be prepared during the session.

Play games that require friends to work together. Some games are suggested on pages 43 and 44.

Snack Recipes

Chocolate Bananas

12 bananas
1 cup powdered sugar
4 tablespoons cocoa

chopped nuts (optional)
whipped cream (optional)

Cut the bananas into four pieces. Roll each section in the mixture of powdered sugar and cocoa. Sprinkle the coated banana with the nuts and top with whipped cream.

Peanut Butter Balls

1 cup peanut butter
1 cup corn syrup
1½ cups powdered nonfat milk
1¼ cups sifted powdered sugar
whole peanuts (optional)

Mix together the ingredients. Roll the mixture into 1½ to 2 inch balls. For variety, put two or three peanuts in the center of each ball.

Fruit Shake

½ orange
¼ banana
1 scoop vanilla ice cream

¼ teaspoon vanilla
1 strawberry
⅛ cup milk

Squeeze the juice from the orange and pour it into a blender. Add the banana, strawberry, vanilla, milk, and ice cream. Blend until smooth. Pour into a glass. Makes one serving.

PB Cookie Balls

¾ cup butter
20 graham crackers
¾ cup peanut butter

Crush the graham crackers in a plastic bag. Pour into a bowl and add the peanut butter and butter. Mix well. Roll into 1-inch balls and place on wax paper to set or eat right away.

Nuts and Bolts

4 cups Rice Chex cereal
4 cups Wheat Chex cereal
4 cups pretzels
1 cup peanuts
Lawry's Seasoning Salt
½ cup margarine

Mix the cereals, pretzels, and peanuts together in a large bowl. Melt the margarine and season to taste with the Lawry's Seasoning Salt. Pour over the dry ingredients, toss lightly, and serve.

 ©1996 by The Standard Publishing Company. Permission is granted to reproduce this page for ministry purposes only—not for resale.

The Friends Game

"The Friends Game" is based on TV's "The Newlywed Game." Choose four pairs of friends to play. The game is designed so that preschoolers as well as adults can answer the questions.

Explain that one friend from each pair will go out of the room while three questions are asked of the other friend. The friend is to answer the way he thinks his friend would answer. Make sure he writes his answer down on paper or poster board. Then the friend will come back into the room and answer the questions. The pair will receive five points for every matching answer. The pairs reverse in the second round. The other friend goes out of the room while three questions plus a 15-point bonus question are being asked. Again, the friend answers the way he thinks his friend would answer. The second friend returns to the room and answers the questions. The pair will receive 10 points for every matching answer. The bonus question is used only in the case of a tie.

Round 1
(5-point questions)
1. What is your friend's favorite color?
2. What activity does your friend enjoy most?
3. How many years have you been friends?

Round 2
(10-point questions)
1. What is your friend's favorite food?
2. When was the first time the two of you did something together?
3. Would your friend rather read, watch TV, or talk?
(15-point bonus question)
Whose foot size is bigger—yours or your friend's?

Spoon Race

Tie a very long piece of string or yarn to several stainless steel spoons. Divide the group into families with their friends. Instruct each family group to lie down on the floor head to foot to head to foot. The object of the game is to run the spoon with the string tied to it through each shirt and pants of the family group. The first group to run the spoon through everyone's clothes wins. The game could be played a second time to remove the spoon.

Stomach Giggle

Guide each family group to lay on each other's stomach and giggle. Lying down on the floor, each person will put their head on another person's stomach. Then everyone giggles.

Jigsaw Puzzles

Provide simple puzzles for the youngest of the friends to work on together.

Number Riddle

Give everyone a piece of paper and pencil. Guide them to follow the instructions in order to solve this riddle. You may want to provide several calculators.

1. Write down your house number.
2. Double it.
3. Add 5.
4. Multiply it by 50.
5. Add your age.
6. Add 365.
7. Subtract 615.
8. Your house number should be on the left and your correct age is on the right.

Pair Stand

Guide friends to sit back-to-back on the floor. Link arms at the elbows. Instruct them to try to stand up.

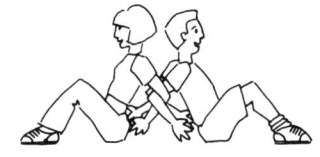

Celebrate Friends

When teaching about making and keeping friends, it is natural to guide your students to celebrate the friends they have. Celebrating those friendships will help them see the value of working to make friends. Celebrating those friendships will also help students take a hard look at the kind of friends they have made. It may be that they need to celebrate the friend and then move on because the friendship is not a godly one.

Some of your students have already worked hard to build a friendship that is important to them. A student may feel as if he has a friend that will be a friend for life. He may be fortunate enough to have a Christian friend that lives in his neighborhood or is in most of his classes at school. Another student may believe that a friendship she has is based on godly principles. Your students will want to honor those friends as they celebrate their friendships.

Your students may have new friends they are very excited about. A student may have a friend that she is just beginning to get to know. Another student may have recently met a friend with whom he has a lot in common and enjoys spending time. Your students will want to celebrate these new friendships also. By thinking about the friendship now, at its beginning, the student may be more prepared to establish it based on godly principles.

Whatever the case, friendships need to be celebrated by your students. Many times our friends have no idea how much they mean to us. We tell other people how important that person is to us. But we may never tell the friend himself.

Encourage your students to let their friends know how much they value their friendship.

On the next few pages, you will find several projects for your students to try. Each project is a way he can celebrate a friend. Guide your students to pick one project to work on in the coming weeks. Some students may want to try several projects with different friends. Then the student should report back to the class when the project is completed. The class can benefit from what the student learns about his friendship. Guide the student to tell what he did, how his friend responded, how it made him feel, how it made his friend feel, and how it impacted the friendship.

Project #1—Friend-in-Hiding

Write each student's name on a slip of paper. Put all of the paper slips in a lunch sack or small gift bag. Instruct each student to pull out a name and check to see who it is. If a student draws his own name, he can return the slip of paper and draw another one. When all the names are drawn, give the students instructions about being a friend-in-hiding.

A friend-in-hiding does nice things for his friend without anyone knowing who he is. He could send a card in the mail. She could make a poster and put it in her friend's front yard. He could call and leave a made-up song to a familiar tune on his family's answering machine. She could make a batch of cookies and ask someone to deliver them. He could write a secret joke message to be decoded by his friend. She could make a special box decorated with stickers and drawings for her friend to store special things in.

The important thing to remember is that the friend-in-hiding does everything in secret. No one knows who their friend-in-hiding is.

Your class could have friends-in-hiding for a short length of time—one month—and then reveal who they are at the next class party. This is a good way for some of the students to get to know each other better. Two students who did not interact in the group may be paired and build a friendship. It may also aid in beginning to break up cliques in your group.

Project #2—One-Half Birthday Party

Encourage each students to choose a friend and give him a one-half birthday party. The party is planned for exactly six months after the friend's birthday. For example, if the friend's birthday is November 29, then her one-half birthday is May 29. The one-half birthday party is just like a birthday party except

that everything is split in half. Friends bring half of a gift. Only half of a birthday cake is served. The one giving the party should be as imaginative as possible.

Everything for the party would be one-half of what it normally is. The invitations could be cut in half before they are placed in the envelope to be mailed. Guests at the party could be instructed to bring one-half of anything as a gift. The invitation could specify gag gifts. Party guests will enjoy creatively thinking about what they will bring as a one-half gift—half of a birthday card, half a bag of candy, half a can of halved tennis balls. The possibilities are limitless.

Once guests arrive, the friends could participate in party games—but only one-half of them at a time. Or, the guests would play one-half of the game. They could play the traditional party games—pin the tail on the donkey, break a pinata. They could play board games or outside games also. The friend giving the party could plan a scavenger hunt for halves of some unusual items—half of a plastic Easter egg, the top half of a hot-dog bun, half of a broken shoe lace. The guests at the party would go door-to-door in the neighborhood asking for the items.

Party favors could be divided in half. All of the food, drinks, and even the birthday cake would be served in halves. Sing only one-half of the Happy Birthday song, "Happy birthday to you. Happy birthday to you. Happy . . ."

The friend who is being honored with the party would feel important. He would realize how special he was to his friend.

Project #3—Friends Journal

Your students may want to keep a journal about their friendships. Some of your students may already keep a diary. They would enjoy this activity. Journaling will aid a student in deciding if the friendship he is writing about is one that he should nurture or not.

Writing about a friendship and then reading about it later will make a student realize that the friendship is not based on godly principles. He may discover that he has been with that particular friend every time he gets in trouble at school. He may decide to work harder on some other friendships that he realizes are worth nurturing.

Writing about friendships will also encourage the student to see how important having friends really is. He may grow to appreciate the people in his day-to-day interactions.

Students can use photocopies of page 49 for their journals. They could hole-punch the page to fit in a colorful three ring binder. A student could write in her journal every day or just

Materials
photocopies of page 49

when she feels like she has something to say. Encourage the students to go back and read their journal several times over the next few months. That is how they will learn more about themselves and their patterns in making friends.

Project #4—Friend Day

The students who select this activity to complete will designate a day to celebrate one friend all day. The student will pick a friend and plan ways to make it "her day" all day.

If Linda is the friend chosen, her friend would let her know the night before or early in the morning that "Today is Linda Day."

The friend would plan ways to honor Linda all day long. She could plan acts of kindness, cards, balloons, flowers, surprises, special meals. Anything goes. Here are some examples.

• Ask an older sibling to pick her up for school in a car decorated with a poster and streamers.

• Have a flower or a balloon delivered to the school during the first class.

• Arrange for someone to escort her during the day, carrying her books or book bag.

• Write her a poem or song to tell her how much you appreciate her friendship.

• Get permission for a pizza and sodas to be delivered to Linda in the school cafeteria at lunch time.

• Hide nice notes in her books, locker, coat pockets.

• Arrange for the principal to make an announcement over the loud speaker about your friendship with Linda. Maybe he would read a poem you wrote about her.

• Present Linda with a memory book you put together, showing or telling about some of the things you have done as friends.

We met when

This friendship is special to me because

One of our favorite things to do together is

I remember the time . . .

We had a disagreement when

Other things I want to write about our friendship

Dear God, please bless my friendship with _____. She/he is very special to me because

I would like our friendship to be more like a godly friendship by

My Friend Journal

My Friendship with

 ©1996 by The Standard Publishing Company. Permission is granted to reproduce this page for ministry purposes only—not for resale.

Unit 2

The Wonder Years

Families have been around since God created Adam and Eve. The family unit can and has been everything from a source of comfort and safety to a place of hurt and anger. Families are something everyone has in common, but seldom are two alike.

During the past fifty years or so, families have gone under enormous change. Dr. James Dobson states in his book, *Children at Risk,* "In 1960, everyone knew that a family meant a husband and wife with or without children. The law defined it a bit more broadly, as people related by blood, marriage, and adoption. Most children were cared for by their parents, and most politicians knew that any effort to strengthen the family was a good idea. In 1990, politicians can't even agree on what 'traditional' families are or whether they are worthy of special assistance. Indeed, a major movement is underway to redefine 'family' to mean any group of people which merely thinks of itself as family."

This change in assumptions has many implications for all families. Because of the rise in the number of divorces and single parent families, childhood is changing. United States Census records show that over 1.25 million divorces occur each year. That is about 150 an hour! About 70 of these divorces involve parents with children under 18 years of age. That means that about twice a minute in this country, a child has his or her family broken up.

Obviously this has affected church families as well. Several years ago churches rarely included divorced or step families. Now, in some areas, they are a large part of the congregation.

Session 1
Know God's guidelines for families
Feel secure in God's love and grace.
Accept and **strengthen** your family.

Session 2
Know that seeing things from another's viewpoint shows God's love.
Feel committed to harmony and unity with siblings.
Begin to put others before self.

Session 3
Know that children cannot cause or prevent divorce.
Feel compassion toward anyone in a divorce situation.
Live according to biblical principles no matter what the family situation.

Session 4
Know that children fear the unknown and can feel isolated in times of crisis.
Feel confidence from God's presence in troubled times.
Develop a plan that will help handle crisis by implementing appropriate behavior.

It is difficult for children to live in a family where parents aren't happy together. Adjustment to life in a single parent home and/or traveling back and forth between parents is also difficult. Later when a stepparent and step siblings are added, it can seem to the child as if what he needs or wants is no longer of importance. The child will find it disconcerting to be told that he is getting a new stepparent and at the same time new brothers and/or sisters. The child is expected to love these virtual strangers and treat them as family.

Life has changed in other ways for preteens in this generation. Crisis in families is more prevalent today. Children face abuse, addictions, neglect, and death of grandparents and parents. It is difficult for the preteen to develop coping skills for the crises they may face.

Television and the media chip away at moral values and principles. What preteens learn at home or at church can be in direct conflict with what they see portrayed as everyday life in the media.

This series of sessions will equip those who choose to work with preteens, to meet their needs through activities that take into account their age and development.

Strong families, however, take work on everyone's part. It is important for the child to have a place to vent his feelings and thoughts, but it is also important that he begin to accept responsibility in his own family. The sessions will give opportunities for discussion about families and will help preteens apply biblical principles in their homes. At the conclusion of these sessions, the preteen will have a biblical standard to measure his own responses to his family. Not every problem has an easy remedy or solution, but a solid faith in God and in His Word can give a firm foundation in the midst of difficult times.

The titles for the sessions are television show titles. This was done to reflect the pervasive influence television has on our culture. Television families are sometimes used as role models for family life. Equipping preteens to discern what should be used as a family role model is a worthy goal for these sessions. As stated earlier, there is no way to completely address and answer all concerns in these four topics. But it is important for the preteen to be aware of his own current reactions to family events and changes. He can learn to measure his ideas against God's standard. It can lay the groundwork for a response that is Christlike when faced with family conflict.

The **Bridge the Gap** session builds upon the truths learned in the four sessions. During the **Take It to the Next Level** section at the end of each session, students will have an opportunity to work on a "family album." The students are encouraged to investigate their own family and discover new information about their parents, grandparents, and other ancestors. To culminate the unit, the class celebrates families by hosting a "family reunion" party or picnic. The activities will include sharing information from the family albums. There will also be a time for games that the families can do together. This is one small way to encourage and celebrate family togetherness.

The **Go to Extremes** service, "A Family for All Seasons," includes four service project options—one for each season. You may choose an option depending on the time of year you are using this material. Or you may choose an option that would best fit the needs of your group. Each activity is designed to involve parents and students working together in the project. Almost all of the activities can be modified to work in any season, so you may decide to do another option later in the year. In Spring, families can work to "Spruce up the Neighborhood" by doing home repair for others in their church or community who are unable to do so. In Summer, plan a "Family Fair" carnival as an outreach to the community. In Autumn, "Senior Saint's Day" involves a visit to a nursing or retirement home. And in Winter, "Adopt a Family" by providing food and toys to other less-fortunate families in your area who may need extra care during the holidays.

Devotional Thoughts for the Leader

Session 1

Read Ephesians 6:14. Although verse 4 refers to fathers it can also be applied to the role of a teacher. We want to train and instruct the children in the Lord. Spend time in prayer thanking God for the opportunity to teach children and also pray for the children in the class to have open ears and hearts.

Session 2

Read Psalm 133. David used this in context of relating to godly people, but it can pertain to sibling relationships as well. Pray, expressing thanksgiving for family units and for the preteen's sibling relationships.

Session 3

Read Romans 12:14-21. These are good things to remember in all relationships, but especially in regard to divorce and remarriage. Thank God for real examples of relationships. Ask Him to help the students put others before themselves.

Session 4

Read Psalm 139. This beautiful Psalm reminds us that God does care for us and knows what we're going through. Thank God for His comfort and ask Him to help the students in your class feel comfortable to share from their hearts.

(The authors would like to acknowledge Brian Davis, Mike Tuttle, Mike Thompson, and Julie Katzman's 5th grade for their assistance.)

Family Ties

Scripture. Genesis 1:27, 28; Mark 10:7, 8

Know God's guidelines for families.
Feel secure in God's love and grace.
Accept and **strengthen** your family.

Get Into the Game

It is sometimes difficult for children to share personal information and feelings. This activity will help break the ice while at the same time share information about their individual families.

To begin, distribute a copy of the reproducible sheet "Family" and a pencil to each student. Tell the students that they will have two minutes to collect as many different signatures as possible on their "bingo" sheets. This will enable them to get to know something about everyone in the class. If your class is small, tell students that names may be repeated.

At the end of the two minutes, bring students back into one group. Go over the sheets, allowing students the opportunity to reveal interesting information about their families. After you have determined a winner, award him or her with a small prize.

Tell students that over the next few weeks they will be studying and evaluating families. They will also be finding new ways to strengthen and support their own families.

Materials
photocopies of page 57, pens or pencils, small prize (optional)

Step 1

To begin introducing the topic of families, ask the students, "What do you think of when you hear the word family?"

Allow the students to think about and discuss the question. Then say, "Let's find out what others—including God—think about families." Divide the class into three groups. Each group will be given one of the following activities to work on.

Activity #1—Media's View of the Family

Start a discussion about television families by handing out a copy of "Family Matters" to each child. Have students list TV shows that focus on families (i.e. "Home Improvement," "Family Matters," etc.). Have them answer the two questions for each television show they have listed.

Next, let them list all their answers on the poster board. Compare the way TV families are shown to their own families.

Materials
photocopies of page 58, pens or pencils, poster board, markers

Do TV shows really represent the way families act? Add some of these responses to the poster board.

Activity #2—Church Members' View of Family

Tell students that they are going to be investigative reporters. Make "press passes" by writing the word "reporter" on a card and attaching it to a chain, cord, or string for each child to wear. Tell students they will be using video recorders (or tape recorders) to interview people. (Make sure you have made contact with several people to be available for this segment.) Reporters copy these three questions on an index card, to ask each church member:

1. What is a family?
2. What positive things can happen in a family?
3. What negative things can happen in a family?

Ask the students, based on their interviews, to give a short summary statement on what a family is. They can write these responses on the poster board provided. The students could evaluate the comments that were made by listing qualities and/or characteristics that are found in families.

Materials
video or audio tape recorders, index cards with the word "reporter" written on them, paper, pencils, poster board titled "Our Views," markers, two or three church members (contacted before class), questions written on index cards

Activity #3—God's View of the Family

Give students the index cards with Scripture references written on them. Have students look up the Scriptures and take turns reading them aloud in this order: Mark 10:6-9; Genesis 1:27, 28; Ephesians 6:1-3; Colossians 3:20; 1 Peter 3:8, 9; and Philippians 2:14, 15.

With those verses in mind, lead a discussion based on the following suggestions. Divide the poster board into three sections. Number the sections 1-3 and write the group's response in the appropriate area.

1. What was God's initial pattern for marriage and family? (i.e. one man, one woman, children). At this point, even if your class is made up of children in traditional families, mention that not all families are like this. Some children live with just one parent, some live with stepparents, some live with grandparents, and some are adopted. Explain that God's standard revealed in the Bible provides the best guidance for families. God understands this is not always the case. People who love and work at serving the Lord do not follow God's will perfectly. God loves and helps single-parent families or stepfamilies, too. When we ask, God forgives our mistakes—even mistakes that involve whole families. God can help make every family stronger because He loves His people so much.

2. What instructions does God give families, especially children? (Obey your parents, live in harmony, and do not complain or argue.)

Materials
index cards with Scriptures written on them, Bibles, poster board titled "God's View," markers

3. How can you follow the instructions? (Get along with parents and/or siblings, do chores without being reminded, etc.)

Step 2

As each group finishes its activities, have them reassemble into one large group.

Begin by allowing the students from Activity #1 to present the results of their media study. Ask the students, "Can you think of any other television programs that center around families? How realistic are these programs?" Allow students the opportunity to discuss these programs, then encourage them to examine all the television they watch according to biblical standards.

Next, invite the students involved in Activity #2 to present their findings to the rest of the class. If the students used video or audio recorders, provide the equipment necessary for the presentation, offering assistance when needed. When the students have finished, ask the rest of the group the same questions: "What is a family?" (A father and/or mother with one or more children.) "What positive and/or negative things can happen in a family?" (Some possible answers include someone to talk to, someone to spend time or play with, someone to get advice from, someone to share your room with, someone who fights with you, someone who can be jealous of you, someone who can hurt or abuse you.)

Finally, allow the students who participated in Activity #3 to present their poster board. Have students again read the Scripture references before going over their results. Encourage students who were not involved in this activity to add to the poster board answers. Encourage the students to commit at least one of the Scripture references to memory.

Step 3

To give students an opportunity to move around and apply some of the principles they've learned, play the following game. Have them stand in a circle and extend their arms toward the middle of the circle. Each student needs to grab the hand of two people. Make sure they do not have the hand of someone who is directly next to them. Without letting go of hands, the children need to untangle themselves until a circle is formed again. This means some may need to step over hands or go under hands. Once this has been completed, have the children talk about how they felt (frustrated, angry, dumb, excited), what was needed to get the job accomplished (teamwork, someone taking charge, patience), and how it relates to life in a family (frustrated when people won't listen to you, have to stick with it to the end, problems can be solved by working together).

Take It to the Next Level

Read Proverbs 20:11. Based on this and the others Scriptures studied in this session, have students consider what they can do this week to improve their individual families (i.e. do what parents ask the first time, don't argue with siblings or parents).

Tell students that over the course of this study on families, they will be making family albums. Each student will add new material to an album at the end of each session.

Distribute notebooks, pens, and three-hole punched paper to each student. Tell students to take one piece of paper and write "Family Pledge" at the top. Each week the students will list an activity that they promise to work at for improving their families.

Tell them to think about their Proverbs 20:11 discussion and write one thing as #1. Some possibilities include: make my bed or clean my room without being asked, offer to do a specific chore that someone else in the family usually does, pray for parent(s) every day.

Distribute copies of the "Family Word Search" puzzle for students to take home and complete. This can be added to their albums. If time remains, allow students to decorate their family albums with markers or stickers. Remind them to bring the albums back to the next session. (If you think they will forget them, keep the notebooks in the classroom for next week.)

Close in prayer, thanking God for the guidelines He has set for families. You may want to ask students for prayer requests pertaining to their families.

Materials

notebooks or pocket folders for each student, three-hole punched paper, pens or pencils, markers, photocopies of page 82 in the family session, stickers (optional)

FAMILY

My father works as a _____.	I have a birthday this month.	I have a pet dog.	I have more than one sister at home.	I have one sister at home.	I was born in this state.
My mother works as a _____.	Someone in my family has a birthday this month.	I have a pet cat.	I have more than one brother at home.	I have one brother at home.	I was born in another state.
I have grandparents living in _____.	I had a birthday last month or will have a birthday next month.	I have a pet that is *not* a dog or cat.	I have at least one younger brother or sister.	I have no brothers or sisters.	I was born in another country.

 ©1996 by The Standard Publishing Company. Permission is granted to reproduce this page for ministry purposes only—not for resale.

Family Matters

List one TV family on each TV screen. Answer these questions for each one.

1. How does this family compare to my own family?

2. Does this family show the way families really act? Why or why not?

58 ©1996 by The Standard Publishing Company. Permission is granted to reproduce this page for ministry purposes only—not for resale.

Home Improvement

Scripture. Ephesians 5:1, 2; 1 John 4:19-21; James 1:19; Psalm 133:1; 1 Peter 3:8, 9; Philippians 2:14, 15a

Know that seeing things from another's viewpoint shows God's love.
Feel committed to harmony and unity with siblings.
Begin to put others before self.

Get Into the Game

To open this session, ask the students, "What was the last fight you had with a *sibling?*" (Note: you may need to define the word sibling.) Allow the students time to respond. Then ask, "Who was 'in the right' in your fight?"

Tell the class that they'll be part of an experiment related to how to answer that question. Have the tray prepared ahead of time and covered with a towel. Set the table up in an adjacent room or in the hallway with the tray on it. Use masking tape to number each side of the table 1-4. Have the students number off in fours. Take four students with a different number, and have them stand by their corresponding number on the table. Have them kneel and rest their chins on the number in front of them. Uncover the items and have the four students stare at the tray for one minute. Have those students return to their seats and write on a piece of paper what items they saw on the tray. Give them only one minute to write their list, then collect the lists. It is important for them *not* to talk to anyone else at this time. While they are writing, have another set of four students come to the table and repeat the process until all have had a chance to make their list. (If you have more than twelve students or three groups, recruit a helper. Prepare two trays and tables and carry out the process two groups at a time.)

Regroup the students into four groups according to their number—the numbers on the sides of the table. Have each group discuss the list of things they wrote. Have a representative from each group list three things they saw from their side of the table. (Obviously, no one group will be able to list all objects found on the tray.) Show them the tray and name all of the objects on it. Discuss why the four lists are different. Some responses you may receive are: "We couldn't see the whole thing"; "You wouldn't let me raise my chin and see the rest"; "We didn't have enough time."

Materials

a tray with 15-20 items that differ in height, depth, width (i.e. scissors, pop can, stapler, paper clip, ribbon, etc.); a towel to cover the tray; square table (card table); masking tape; markers; paper; pencils

Guide them to conclude that they were limited because they only saw one view of the tray. Explain that sometimes we do that in relationships too. We look at situations only from our point of view and never consider another's point of view. Refer back to the earlier discussion about the fight they had with a sibling. Ask if they see what the sibling may have been thinking during the fight.

Step 1

Divide the students into three groups. Each group will work on a specific activity that they will present to the rest of the class in the Step 2 portion of this session.

Activity #1

This group will study the story of Joseph and present it to the other class members as a verse, song, or rap.

If students are not familiar with the story of Joseph, have them look up and read marked portions of Genesis 35, 37, 41, 42, and 45. Encourage them to write specific events in the story, from Joseph's receiving the coat of many colors to the brothers' reunion in Egypt.

Ask the following questions: "What was the perspective of Joseph's brother's?" (jealousy, envy) "What was Joseph's response when the brother's came to Egypt?" (In the end, he did not hold a grudge; he forgave his brothers, and the family was reunited.)

When you feel the students are comfortable with the facts of Joseph's story have them work together as a group, in pairs, or individually (depending on the size) to write a song, verse, or rap about Joseph. Encourage them to include the lesson to be learned from this story. A sample rap is provided.

Materials
Bible, pencils, paper

The Joseph Jam

Now Joseph was the kid with the coat of many colors.
He got it from his dad, and it really bugged his brothers.
See they thought that dear old dad just wasn't playin' fair,
So they started up a plan to get Joseph out of there.

The brothers couldn't take it—
they burned with jealousy.
So they sold him to some travelers,
Into slave-er-ry.

But Joseph did OK,
He overcame the schemes.

He's a VIP in Egypt,
By explainin' Pharaoh's dreams.

Now many years later,
there's a famine in the land.
And the brothers come a knockin'
'cause they need a helping hand.

So Joseph helps his brothers,
and the group is reunited.
They pack and move to Egypt—
That makes Joseph's dad excited!

So the moral to the story,
as you can plainly see—
Don't hold a grudge, forgive, forget,
then live in harmony.

Tell the students to rehearse their songs and be ready to perform them for the rest of the class later in the session.

Activity #2

Make sure all the students have an NIV Bible. Explain that you will be having a contest (sometimes referred to as a sword drill) to see who can find a Bible book, chapter, and verse the quickest. Once a contestant finds the correct verse, he stands up. Have that student put a book mark at the verse until all the verses have been found. Ephesians 5:1, 2; 1 John 4:19-21; James 1:19; Psalm 133:1; I Peter 3:8, 9; Philippians 2:14, 15a. After contestants have found all the Scriptures, have them read and discuss them one by one. Discuss the following questions: What advice did you hear in this verse? What would your relationships with your siblings be like if you followed the advice in this verse? Make a list of good advice for getting along with siblings.

Materials
Bible

Activity #3

Distribute a copy of the "Secret Bible Verse" puzzle to each student. Help the students follow the directions to discover the "Secret Bible Verse" (Psalm 133:1).

Tell students that within the next week they need to do something special (and if possible in secret) for one or more of their siblings. They should choose something that the other person would really like. It might not be something they would appreciate having done for themselves. If one of the students doesn't have a sibling, they could do something for a parent or close friend. For example, they could make a bed, do a chore,

Materials
photocopies of page 64, pencils

or buy a favorite candy bar. By actually doing something like this it will help the students to think about another's perspective. (Note: A normal reaction from the class may be complaining and groaning. If you think it is appropriate, stress to the students that as we study the Bible, God expects us to take what we have read and learned and apply it to our lives.)

Step 2

As each group finishes its activity, have the students come together in one large group. Tell the students, "Sometimes getting along with your brothers and sisters isn't easy. It's been that way at least since this Old Testament story happened."

At this time, ask the students involved with Activity #1 to perform their songs. When they have finished say, "Joseph and his brothers had some tough times, but their story has a happy ending. How would you have responded if you had been Joseph?" Allow time for response. "We all may want to get even at times, but the Bible tells us the way we should respond."

Next, let the students involved with Activity #2 read the Scriptures aloud. Ask the students, "Can you think of a situation with a brother or sister that might have turned out differently if you had known these verses?" Give the students a chance to respond.

Finally, let the students involved with Activity #3 present their puzzles and tell the one thing they will do for their siblings in the next week. Encourage all the students to be thinking of things they could do for their siblings in the coming week.

Step 3

Tell students to return to their previous groups of three and distribute copies of "Sibling Situations." Assign each group one of the situations and have them decide on a way to act it out. Encourage them to come up with a realistic ending.

Materials
photocopies of the reproducible page 65

1. Two of you, after talking with each other, have discovered that your older brother has been going through your personal things in your room (letter, diary, etc.). How do you deal with this?

2. Your sister always gets good grades in school. Your parents don't understand why you can't do as well as your sister. They are constantly holding her up as an example. How do you deal with this?

3. Your younger sister is allowed to watch her favorite program on TV after school. Today there is an after-school special that you would really like to see. Your sister has just turned on her program. How do you deal with this?

4. The kids in your neighborhood have decided to have a ball game at the park. You have been invited to go and look for your baseball glove and bat in the garage. You can't find them. Later that week, you find out that your younger brother took it to camp with him. How do you deal with this?

5. There is a boy in your class who likes you, and he knows you have a younger brother. The boy who likes you has been asking your brother questions about you and sharing the information with others in your class. How do you deal with this?

Once each group has had an opportunity to discuss the situation, they need to act it out for the rest of the class. Try not to help the students too much. This will allow you to see how much they have learned from the session.

Take It to the Next Level

With the remaining time, allow students to work on their family albums. Tell them to add a second promise to the Family Pledge sheet. Encourage them to word this pledge so it will pertain to siblings. Remind them of the day's session and have them think of one way they could each be a better brother or sister.

When they're finished, distribute copies of the "Family Questionnaire" on page 81. Students will answer these questions at home, then add them to their albums. Also, encourage students to ask their parent or parents for some family photos they can add to the albums.

Close the session with a prayer circle, asking students to pray silently for specific family situations. Pray aloud that students will be slow to anger and arguments when dealing with their siblings.

Materials
photocopies of page 81

Do the math problem and then find the letter that corresponds to the number.

12 ÷ 12 = □
7 + 5 = □
24 ÷ 12 = □
1 x 3 = □
6 x 2 = □
11 + 1 = □
16 - 6 = □
14 + 3 = □
14 ÷ 3 = □
5 x 1 = □

15 ÷ 5 = □
4 x 5 = □
15 - 12 = □
14 - 7 = □
1 x 2 = □
12 + 5 = □
4 + 4 = □
21 ÷ 3 = □
3 x 3 = □
6 + 1 = □

7 + 4 = □
19 - 7 = □
18 ÷ 1 = □
31 ÷ 8 = □
1 + 0 = □
17 - 14 = □
22 ÷ 2 = □
40 ÷ 10 = □
2 x 10 = □
7 + 1 = □
19 - 5 = □
18 ÷ 6 = □

1 + 1 = □
15 - 14 = □
27 ÷ 9 = □
1 x 2 x 1 = □

16 - 13 = □
6 + 1 = □
6 x 2 = □
36 ÷ 6 = □
33 ÷ 11 = □
16 - 9 = □
13 ÷ 13 = □
24 - 21 = □
6 + 5 = □

36 ÷ 4 = □
24 ÷ 3 = □
11 + 11 = □
19 - 11 = □
3 x 3 x 1 = □
42 ÷ 6 = □
13 x 1 = □

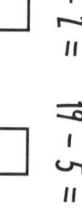

A	B	C	D	E	F	G	H	I	J	K	L	M	N	O	P	Q	R	S	T	U	V	W	X	Y	Z
17	13	15	10	3	16	6	1	9	18	19	20	21	8	12	5	23	11	4	7	22	14	2	24	16	15

64   ©1996 by The Standard Publishing Company. Permission is granted to reproduce this page for ministry purposes only—not for resale.

Sibling Situations

1 Two of you, after talking with each other, have discovered that your older brother has been going through your personal things in your room (letter, diary, etc.). How do you deal with this?

2 Your sister always gets good grades in school. Your parents don't understand why you can't do as well as your sister. They are constantly holding her up as an example. How do you deal with this?

3 Your younger sister is allowed to watch her favorite program on TV after school. Today there is an after-school special that you would really like to see. Your sister has just turned on her program. How do you deal with this?

4 The kids in your neighborhood have decided to have a ball game at the park. You have been invited to go and look for your baseball glove and bat in the garage. You can't find them. Later that week, you find out that your younger brother took it to camp with him. How do you deal with this?

5 There is a boy in your class who likes you, and he knows you have a younger brother. The boy who likes you has been asking your brother questions about you and sharing the information with others in your class. How do you deal with this?

 ©1996 by The Standard Publishing Company. Permission is granted to reproduce this page for ministry purposes only—not for resale.

Step by Step

Scripture. Mark 10:2-9; Genesis 1:27, 28

Know that children cannot cause or prevent divorce.
Feel compassion toward anyone in a
divorce situation.
Live according to biblical principles no
matter what the family situation.

Get Into the Game

This activity will help the students develop interdependence.
Divide your class into pairs. Give each pair two handfuls of
mini-marshmallows (substitute Legos or blocks if desired) and
a blindfold. Explain to the class that one person will need to
put on the blindfold. The other person will be giving instructions for building a tower with the marshmallows to resemble
the model that you will show them in a few moments. Once
all the blindfolds are in place, unveil or bring out the model.
Give the students five minutes to complete their own model.
Have the student who is blindfolded remove it and see how
closely it matches your model. Repeat the activity with the
person who was blindfolded giving instructions. (You may
want to change the model you have to be more challenging
for the second group.) Again, give them five minutes to complete the activity. Bring everyone back into a group setting and
debrief. "How did you feel when you were the one blindfolded? Did you *need* your partner to give you instructions to build
it? How did you feel when you were giving instructions? Were
you frustrated when your partner didn't do what you told him
(or couldn't understand what you meant)?" Allow time for
response.

"Some people live with a stepparent. Many people have stepbrothers or sisters and/or half-brothers or sisters. We are going
to spend some time discussing, learning, and looking at these
relationships. Even if your family is not affected by divorce and
remarriage, by the end of this session, the tower you built with
your partner's help will help you remember some important
keys to understanding divorce."

Materials
mini-marshmallows, Legos blocks or
other building materials, blindfolds,
model of a tower, covering for model

Step 1

The three activities in Step 1 are designed to inform students
about types of families that can develop from divorce, typical
reactions towards divorce, and the Bible's comments on
divorce.

Activity #1

This group will be working on a poster that presents the different types of families they may be familiar with. Before class, write the following definitions on individual index cards.

1. Adoptive Family. A father and mother who have permanent legal custody of a child who is not their biological child. Birth parents are called biological parents.

2. Blended Family. A parent and a stepparent who have children from another marriage. Sometimes only one parent has children. Sometimes both people have children. The brothers or sisters who belong to the stepparent are called your stepbrothers or stepsisters. If your parent and stepparent have a new baby, the baby is your half-brother or half-sister.

3. Foster Family. Adults who provide care for part of a child's life. They love, protect, and provide for the children as if they were their own.

4. Nuclear Family. A father and mother and their biological children.

5. Single Parent Family. A father or mother and his or her biological children.

Have the students read the definitions, being certain that they understand them. Then have the students find pictures in magazines to represent these families. For example, pictures of adopted or foster families could include children of a different race than the parents. Have students glue the pictures to the poster board and write the names under each family represented.

Materials
magazines, poster board, glue sticks, scissors, markers, index cards with definitions written on them

Activity #2

Distribute copies of "What Would You Say?" to each student. Have the students read the situations and write one possible reaction for each one. Encourage students to write an honest response without worrying whether or not they're giving a "right" answer. Tell students to prepare to read their responses to the rest of the class during Step 2.

Materials
photocopies of page 71, pens or pencils

Activity #3

This group will look to the Bible and see what God says about divorce. Read the following to the students, taken from the *Kids' Application Bible.* (If you cannot locate this version, use the *New International Version.*) Mark 10:2-9 says, "Some Pharisees came and asked him, 'Do you permit divorce?' Of course they were trying to trap him. 'What did Moses say about divorce?' Jesus asked them. 'He said it was all right,' they replied. 'He said that all a man has to do is write his wife a letter of dismissal.' 'And why did he say that?' Jesus asked. 'I'll tell you why—it was a concession to your hardhearted wicked-

Materials
Bibles, bookmarks

ness. But it certainly isn't God's way. For from the very first he made man and woman to be joined together permanently in marriage; therefore, a man is to leave his father and mother, and he and his wife are united so that they are no longer two, but one. And no man may separate what God has joined together.'"

Lead the students in a discussion about the Scripture just read. Ask the following: "What is God's intent for marriage and family?" (Mark 10:7, 8 and Genesis 1:27, 28) "How long is marriage to last?" (forever—Mark 10:9) Remind students of the Scripture discussion from the first session of this unit. God is pleased when families follow the biblical standard, but He understands this is not the case, just as not everyone keeps God's standard in other areas of life. When asked, God will forgive mistakes and help make families, whatever their situation, stronger just as God helps and forgives us when we make mistakes.

When adults make choices that affect us, we are not responsible for those choices. (If you did not present Session 1, you may want to look over that particular section and add the Scripture to this lesson.)

There are some things that the students can *remember* when going through family problems. Provide several NIV Bibles. Before class label the following verses with a bookmark (one for each Bible): Psalm 27:10, 11a; Matthew 11:28, 29; 1 Peter 5:7. Have each verse read then ask how the verses make them feel. Remember, God has promised us that He will be with us in all kinds of situations. Remember, when it seems as if no one else will listen or care, God will always be there.

Likewise, there are things the children can do to be able to get past the rough times. Have the class look up 2 Timothy 2:1, 3 and Romans 12:18. With these verses in mind, ask them what they could do to carry out these verses. Ask them to be as specific as possible.

Recall the tower-building process. The people who were blindfolded could not see the model and needed their partner to help them. Likewise, a child may not be able to or want to see the "whole picture" of a situation (like divorce) and will need help. Preteens can help other preteens, even when neither one can see the whole picture. To finish the model, it was also necessary for the builder to depend on his partner. And it is necessary to depend on others when they are going through rough times. The church family and friends can be a big support during this period. It is important for the children, especially those from divorced and stepfamilies, to begin to understand that although the divorce is not their fault and their parent(s) may not do what the child believes is right, they still need to honor their parents. And the actions they take need to be godly actions—even if this means learning to get along and live with a difficult stepparent or sibling.

Step 2

After all the groups have finished their activities, have them reassemble into one large group.

Let Group 1 come to the front of the room and present their family definitions and poster. When this group has finished, remind the class that all families are unique and special. They may not be able to choose what kind of family they live with, but they can please God by making the best of their situations.

Next, let Group 2 come forward and present the situations. After the students read each situation, allow time for the other class members to respond. Compare their reactions to the ones written down by Group 2. Tell the students, "It's not always easy to know how we should respond in these situations. Sometimes we may feel as if everyone is against us. But Group 3 is going to tell us what God has to say about that."

Let Group 3 come to the front. First have a student read Mark 10:2-9. After the Scripture is read, say, "God doesn't like divorce, but He knows it will happen. He is there for us when we feel lonely and confused." Have students read Psalm 27:10, 11; Matthew 11:28, 29; and 1 Peter 5:7. Tell the students, "God will never abandon us—we can take comfort in that!"

Step 3

As the students in Group 3 return to their seats, pull out the bag of inflated balloons you've prepared ahead of time. Each balloon will contain one of the following words:

Materials
balloons, slips of paper with words written on them, one push pin, garbage bag

Afraid	**Frustrated**
Angry	**Guilty**
Confused	**Jealous**
Depressed	**Lonely**
Disappointed	**Neglected**

If your class has more than ten students, you may want to add more feelings and balloons to the collection. One by one, have a student come forward, pop a balloon with a push pin, and read the word found inside. Then have each student answer the following questions: "How could this feeling relate to a divorce situation? How could God help me with this feeling?" Some possible answers to the first question are as follows:

1. Afraid—that parents will divorce; that parents don't love them.

2. Angry—that their family is changing; that parents would do this to their children.

3. Confused—why their parents don't love them anymore.

4. Depressed—because things have changed; they may not get to see their mother or father as much.

5. Disappointed—in their parents for making mistakes.

6. Frustrated—that they can't fix the situation.

7. Guilty—feeling as if they somehow caused the situation.

8. Jealous—of a new stepmother, stepfather, or step siblings.

9. Lonely—missing the parent that moved out.

10. Neglected—one parent may forget to call or spend time with you.

The answer to the second question can be answered by reviewing the Scriptures discussed in the session. It should be noted that all of the feelings listed are valid—except for guilt. Remind students that children are *not* responsible for their parents' divorce or their decisions.

The students may ask questions about the changes in their family and how to accept them. They may also be experiencing anger, guilt, frustration, added responsibility, and depression. Encourage the children to talk about their feelings, especially to their parents (whether one or both).

Take It to the Next Level

Close this session in prayer. You could thank God for the instructions that help us deal with our families, and for the church family that helps and supports us. Also include a request for guidance and patience as we try to show a Christlike attitude to our family.

Have students continue to work on their family albums. Ask if they were able to go visit their hometown or write for information yet. Encourage those who haven't to do so. They need to have the questionnaire completed by the "family reunion" party. Also send home an invitation to the "family reunion" party for the children and their families.

Make sure students add the third commitment to their Family Pledge sheet. Encourage them to make a pledge based on something they learned in today's session.

What Would You Say?

Read the following situations and write one reaction you might have to each one.

1. Your parents are divorced, and your father constantly puts your mother down by saying negative things about her.

One reaction could be . . .

2. Your parents are divorced, and you and your little sister live with your mother. Mom announces that she is marrying a man with two children. They will be moving in after the wedding.

One reaction could be . . .

3. Your best friend tells you that his parents are getting a divorce, and your friend thinks it is his fault. He wants you to help get them back together.

One reaction could be . . .

 ©1996 by The Standard Publishing Company. Permission is granted to reproduce this page for ministry purposes only—not for resale.

Session 4

Growing Pains

Scripture. Deuteronomy 14:1a; Psalm 139:1-12, 16-18; 2 Corinthians 1:3; James 1:12

Know that children fear the unknown and can feel isolated in times of crisis.

Feel confidence from God's presence in troubled times.

Develop a plan that will help handle crisis by implementing appropriate behavior.

Get Into the Game

Introduce today's topic, facing crisis, by playing a short video clip of a crisis situation. An appropriate video clip can be found by contacting your local chapter of the Red Cross, renting a movie with a crisis scene, or recording a TV segment from a medical or police program. Make sure the scene you choose is appropriate for your particular students. Although preteens often look like teenagers, they can't always discuss situations or draw conclusions as well as teens can. Be sensitive to your class and the maturity level you have observed thus far.

View the clip, then ask the following questions: "How did this scene make you feel?" (scared, upset, nervous, helpless) "If you had been in this situation, what would you have tried to do differently? Could you have changed the outcome? Why or why not?" Allow time for students to think and respond.

After the students have had a chance to discuss what they've seen, explain the purpose of this session. "A crisis can happen to anyone. Although we may not be able to stop a crisis from happening, we can learn how to handle our own reactions and choose what we will do."

Materials
TV and VCR, video clip cued to a crisis situation

Step 1

The activity options in Step 1 are divided into three areas: Identifying Crisis, Preparing for Crisis, and Knowing God's Comfort in Crisis. Divide the students into three groups. Each group will be working on one of the topics mentioned.

Activity #1—Identifying Crisis

The purpose of the activity is to help students identify crisis situations. Distribute copies of "Could This Be a Crisis?" Students will read the situations and answer the questions for each one.

Remind this group that just because one person may view a problem as a crisis doesn't mean everyone would. Nonetheless it would still be a crisis to that person. Sometimes a problem

Materials
photocopies of page 76, pens or pencils

has the potential of becoming a crisis. If that's the case, encourage students to think of ways to stop the problem before it escalates.

Make sure students write their answers on the paper. Remind them to be ready to read their answers to the rest of the class in Step 2.

*Activity #2—*Preparing for Crisis

The purpose of this activity is to help students prepare a resource of phone numbers to be used during crisis situations.

Provide several phone books. Tell the students that they will be compiling a resource list of important phone numbers to be available in case of a crisis.

Distribute photocopies of "Who You Gonna Call?" Have students work as a group to compile their lists. Of course, if your area has 911 service, this is the first number they should list. Have them list numbers for police, firemen, doctors, and nearby hospitals. Have them include numbers for poison control, suicide prevention, Al-a-teen, and any other crisis intervention numbers that are available in your area. You may also want to supply your minister's number, the church office number, and any counselors you feel would be appropriate. Guide the students in completing a well-rounded list.

*Activity #3—*Knowing God's Comfort in Crisis

This activity should help students realize that God doesn't stop bad things from happening to us, but He does promise to offer strength during these times.

Ahead of time, write each Scripture reference on an index card: Deuteronomy 14:1a; Psalm 139:1-2, 16-18; 2 Corinthians 1:3, 4; James 1:12.

Have students work individually or in pairs to locate and read these Scriptures. After they have read them, have the students decide on an answer to the following questions. Write the answers on the back of the card. "How can this Scripture make you feel better during a time of crisis? How can this Scripture help you help someone else who faces a crisis?"

Some possible answers include:

1. Deuteronomy 14:1a. As children of God, we can feel loved even when those who should love us don't act as if they do. No matter how hurt or neglected we may feel, our heavenly Father still cares for us.

2. Psalm 139:1-12, 16-18. Even before we were born, God knew about us and considered us precious. He is with us wherever we are.

3. 2 Corinthians 1:3, 4. Because of God's love, I can be a comfort to a friend or family member in crisis.

Materials
several phone books, photocopies of page 77, pens or pencils

Materials
Bibles, four index cards with a Scripture reference written on them, pens or pencils

4. James 1:12. Although there are trials on earth, God has promised us a time with no troubles or heartache in Heaven. We can rejoice in that.

Help the students if they have trouble answering the questions. Remind them that they will be reading their answers to the rest of the class during Step 2.

Step 2

When all the groups have finished, have them come back together as one large group.

First, allow Group 1 to come forward. Distribute copies of page 76 to the students who did not participate in this activity. As Group 1 reports their answers, have the remaining students write those answers.

When Group 1 has finished, have them return to their seats. Help students summarize with these thoughts: "Someone defined crisis as 'the turning point in the course of anything.' This means that a crisis could actually be a positive thing. Let's look at the first situation as an example. What if your grandfather's chest pains are a sign of stress that could lead to more serious problems. But by discovering it now, your grandpa can be treated with medication to live longer. That would be a case in which the crisis could be helpful. Can you think of other situations like this?" (a tumor found that is benign or can be treated, failing grades that indicate to a teacher the student is having vision or hearing problems) "Now that we've learned how to identify a crisis, let's see what we can do to prepare for it."

Let the students in Group 2 come forward to explain their lists. Distribute copies of page 77 to the students who did not participate in this activity. Encourage students to write the names and numbers down and take them home. Explain, "It's important that we know what to do if a crisis arises. These numbers may come in handy someday. Make sure you keep them in a safe place so you'll always remember where to find them."

After Group 2 sits down, have the students in Group 3 come forward and read their Scriptures. Discuss the questions with the class.

Say, "God never promised that we would live lives free of problems, but He did promise to comfort us during these times. And as the last Scripture suggests, we can help others in times of crisis."

Materials
photocopies of pages 76, 77

Step 3

Have Group 3 return to their seats. Then give each child one strand of thread. Have each child try to break the thread by wrapping it around a finger on each hand and pulling. Next give each student three strands and see if anyone can break the threads.

Read Ecclesiastes 4:9, 10, 12, then ask, "Why could you break one thread but not three? How does this relate to the Ecclesiastes Scripture?" Allow time for responses. "As Christians, God intends for us to help others, and He wants us to seek help when we need it. We should never feel ashamed of going to someone for help, counseling, or advice." (Note: if your group made friendship bracelets in Unit 1, they can recall the strength of the braided cords.)

Materials
three strands of thread for each student, Bible

Take It to the Next Level

Close the session with prayer, thanking God for His comfort and strength during rough times. In the remaining time, have students work on their family albums. By this time, the questionnaires should be completed, and students have acquired some family photos. Have the students mount photos on construction paper with glue or double-stick tape.

Also, have students add their final commitment to their Family Pledge sheet. Make sure the commitment relates to something discussed in today's lesson. This is also a good time to make final preparations for the Family Reunion planned in the **Bridging the Gap** session.

Could This Be a Crisis?

1. When you arrive home after school, your mother tells you she just received a phone call. Your grandfather's been rushed to the hospital complaining of chest pains.

2. Today you noticed that the girl sitting next to you in homeroom has bruises on her arms and legs. When you ask how she got them, she tells you that she fell off of her bike. You remember that she's come to school before with lots of bruises.

3. Progress reports were mailed home this week. When your father opens yours, he discovers that you are failing two classes. He's very upset and demands an explanation.

4. Your best friend gets a new jacket for his birthday. The school bully "accidentally" spills ink on it. Your friend gets angry and threatens to get even after school.

Answer these questions for each situation.

1. Could this become a crisis? (What is the best possible result? worst?)

2. Can you avoid or solve this crisis?

3. If yes, what are three possible ways you can solve it?

4. If no, who could help you avoid or solve this crisis? Name three possibilities.

 ©1996 by The Standard Publishing Company. Permission is granted to reproduce this page for ministry purposes only—not for resale.

Who You Gonna Call?

Phone Number   **Name/Agency**

_____   _____

_____   _____

_____   _____

_____   _____

_____   _____

_____   _____

_____   _____

_____   _____

77   ©1996 by The Standard Publishing Company. Permission is granted to reproduce this page for ministry purposes only—not for resale.

Family Matters

Family time is becoming more and more rare. The busy schedules of all family members make it difficult to spend enough time together. Families rarely live in the same state, let alone the same city anymore. This makes it difficult to get to know grandparents and extended family. This session is designed to help each student investigate his family and to ask questions about his parents and their families. There is also a section that will bring the families of all the students together for a time of relaxation, fun, and learning about each other. The church family is important too, and this will give an opportunity to share with them.

This family session is divided into sections that should be done in conjunction with the four sessions. At the end of each session during the **Take It to the Next Level** section, students will be working on their family albums. By the end of the unit, the albums should be completed and ready to display at the Family Reunion gathering.

Session #1

The students should complete the following at the end of this session:

1. Begin the Family Pledge page by adding the first promise to the sheet (see page 56.)

2. Decorate the covers of their family albums.

3. Take a copy of the "Family Word Search" on page 82 home to complete and add to the album.

Session #2

The students should complete the following at the end of this session:

1. Add the second promise to the Family Pledge sheet.
2. Ask parents for family photos that students can add to their albums.
3. Take a copy of the "Family Questionnaire" found on page 81 home to complete and add to the album.

Session #3

The students should complete the following at the end of this session:

1. Add the third promise to the Family Pledge sheet.
2. Make invitations for the Family Reunion party to take home for their parents.

Session #4

The students should complete the following at the end of this session:

1. Add the final promise to their Family Pledge sheet.
2. Affix the family photos they've acquired to construction paper with glue sticks and add to albums.
3. Add Family Surveys to albums if students have not done so yet.
4. Make last minute preparations for Family Reunion Party.

The Family Reunion Party

Invitations to this party should have been made by the students during Session #2. Determine the dates, time, and place, and have students volunteer to bring a food or beverage item. Make sure all of this information is in the invitation. Each family can bring a food item(s) for the party (just like a family reunion). They could bring things like chips, popcorn, cookies, brownies, vegetables and dip, drink, etc. If your class meets during a season when it is feasible to have a picnic, you could add hamburgers, hot dogs, baked beans, and salads. The party could be held at a park or recreation area if the weather permits.

Decorate the area with picnic-style tablecloths, artificial or real flowers in vases, balloons, citronella candles, and strings of party lights. Have space available to display the family albums. After eating, the families could play games appropriate to the party area (in or out of doors). Indoor games could be: I Spy; Charades; Win, Lose or Draw; or the Human Building Game.

For this last game have the families divide into groups of eight to ten people. Make sure that all family members stay in the same group. It is not essential that the teams be exactly even, but try to come within one or two persons. The teacher will call out the name of an object and each group will need to form that object using all of the people within the group. Give a time limit of five minutes. (You can call time if you see that the groups are finished before the time limit is up.) Have someone prepared to be the judge and they will determine which group has the most "realistic" looking item. Some ideas for objects would be: a boom box, a camera, a television set, a car, a beach, etc. For some of these things you may receive a little resistance from the groups, but encourage them to be creative—you will be amazed at what people come up with.

Outdoor games could include: volleyball, softball or team races. You could do a variation of the three-legged race with all family members connected together. Another suggestion would be to divide the people into two teams. Have each team divide themselves in half with one half going to the other side of the room (at least fifteen feet apart). Have a bat available for each team. The first person begins by holding the bat perpendicular to the ground (with one end touching the ground). They place their right hands on the top of the bat, and at the word "go" spin around five times. As soon as that is completed, they run down to their teammates at the other end of the room (carrying the bat with them). They pass the bat to the person first in that line and continue playing until all members of the team have played once. The first team to complete this wins.

After the games, have the students share their albums. Depending on the time element and the size of your class, you may choose to have only certain things shared. This could be the pictures only, or two or three interesting facts from the questionnaire. You may also have the children decide what they would like to share.

At the end of the party, close with prayer. You may want the group to gather in family units.

Family Questionnaire

Ask your parents and grandparents to help you complete this question-naire. Think of some other things you would like to know about your parents, grandparents, and other relatives and ask those also!

Questions for Your Father

1. Where did you live growing up?

2. What was your favorite board game?

3. Who was your best childhood friend?

4. What is your favorite color? Has it changed over the years?

5. What did you want to be when you grew up?

6. What was your favorite sport?

7. Who is your oldest living relative?

8. How many brothers and sisters do your parents have?

9. What is your favorite childhood holiday memory?

10. What subject did you have trouble with in school?

Questions for Your Grandparents
(father's side)

1. What chores did you have to do growing up?

2. What was your first car? Who paid for it?

3. What was your favorite song when you were a teenager?

4. What was your favorite subject in school?

5. How did your family celebrate holidays (family traditions)?

6. How did you get to school?

7. What is your favorite memory of my mom/dad?

8. Where did you go for your first vacation? How old were you?

9. What is one of your favorite books?

Questions for Your Mother

1. What place(s) did you live while growing up?

2. What was your favorite doll?

3. Who was your best childhood friend?

4. When you were expecting me, what other names did you think about for me?

5. Who is your oldest living relative?

6. How many bothers and sisters do your parents have?

7. What did you want to be when you grew up?

8. What is your favorite childhood holiday memory?

9. What was your favorite game to play as a child?

10. What was your least favorite subject in school? Why?

Questions for Your Grandparents
(mother's side)

1. What chores did you have to do growing up?

2. What was your first car? Who paid for it?

3. What was your favorite song when you were a teenager?

4. What was your favorite subject in school?

5. How did your family celebrate holidays (family traditions)?

6. How did you get to school?

7. What is your favorite memory of my mom/dad?

8. Where did you go for your first vacation? How old were you?

9. What is one of your favorite books?

81 ©1996 by The Standard Publishing Company. Permission is granted to reproduce this page for ministry purposes only—not for resale.

Family Word Search

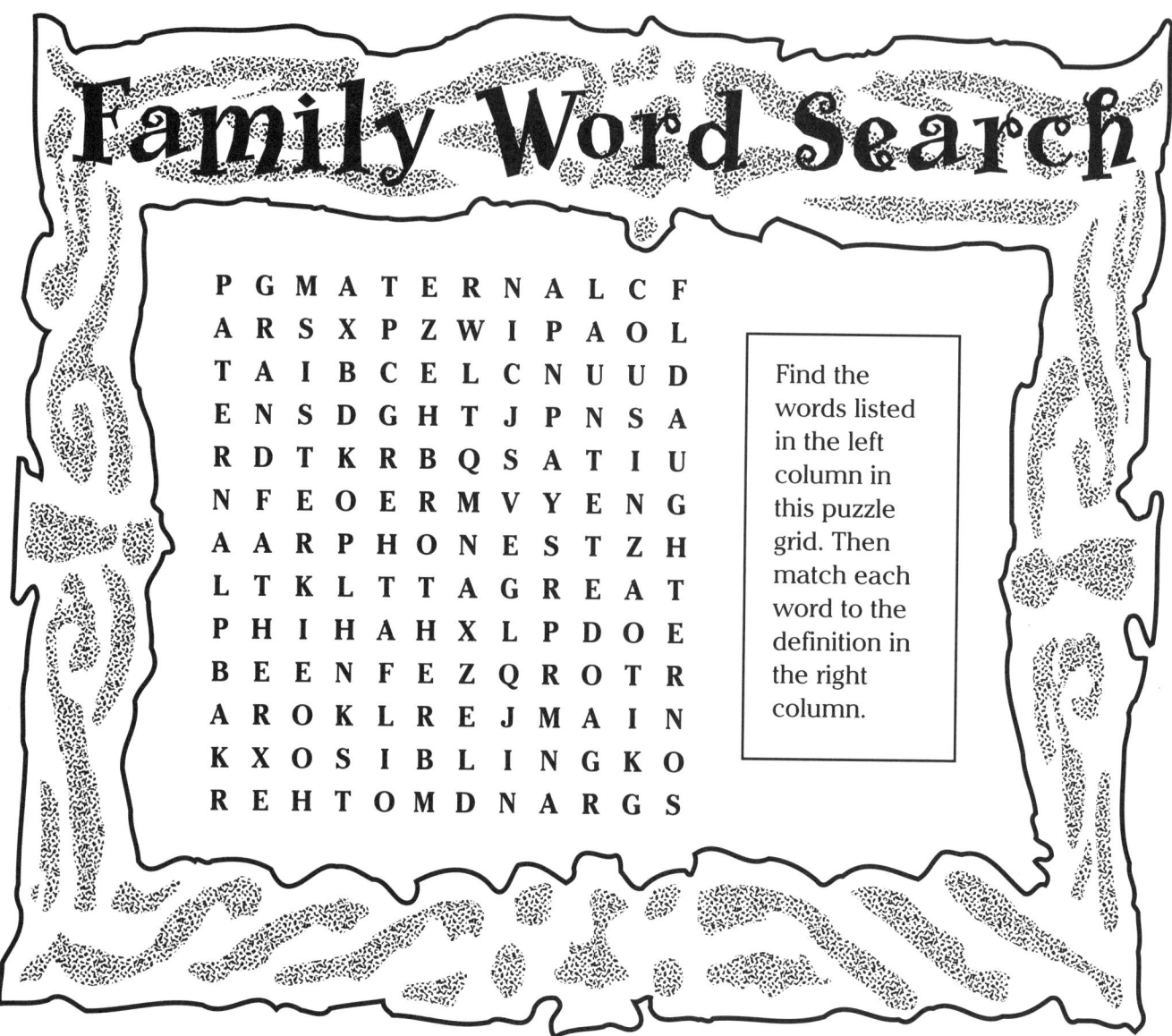

```
P G M A T E R N A L C F
A R S X P Z W I P A O L
T A I B C E L C N U U D
E N S D G H T J P N S A
R D T K R B Q S A T I U
N F E O E R M V Y E N G
A A R P H O N E S T Z H
L T K L T T A G R E A T
P H I H A H X L P D O E
B E E N F E Z Q R O T R
A R O K L R E J M A I N
K X O S I B L I N G K O
R E H T O M D N A R G S
```

Find the words listed in the left column in this puzzle grid. Then match each word to the definition in the right column.

1. Aunt
2. Brother
3. Cousin
4. Daughter
5. Father
6. Grandfather
7. Grandmother
8. Great
9. Maternal
10. Mother
11. Paternal
12. Sibling
13. Sister
14. Son
15. Step
16. Uncle

a. what you call your dad or mom's dad
b. descriptive word used before the word grandmother to describe your grandmother's mother (_____-grandmother)
c. your cousin's dad or your mom or dad's brother
d. term for your mother's side of the family
e. what you call your dad or mom's sister
f. what you call your dad or mom's mother
g. term for brother(s) and/or sister(s)
h. term for your father's side of the family
i. your male parent
j. what you call your uncle or aunt's child
k. your female parent
l. your female sibling
m. descriptive word used before father if your mother remarries
n. your male sibling
o. a female child
p. a male child

82 ©1996 by The Standard Publishing Company. Permission is granted to reproduce this page for ministry purposes only—not for resale.

A Family for All Seasons

This session consists of four separate ideas for service. Each idea is designed around a specific season. Depending on the time of year you study this unit, you may want to select the activity that corresponds to the season. Select any activity you'd prefer and adapt it to fit your season or needs. You may even want to do more than one of these activities!

Although the summer activity is the only one that specifically suggests this, you may want to incorporate help from the students' parents for each project. This will encourage family togetherness.

Autumn—Surprise the Senior Saints

One place that students are always welcome and appreciated is a nursing home or retirement center. The residents often do not see their own family members on a regular basis, and they enjoy seeing and visiting with young people. Students can have an impact on the residents of these places.

Before you take your class to a nursing home or retirement center, prepare ahead for the visit. Well in advance of that day, call the nursing home or retirement center you wish to visit. Ask if they encourage young visitors and if there is a specific day or time that would be better for your group to come and share with the residents. Check with them also to see if there is anything in particular you or your class needs to do or bring. Plan transportation for the group. If your church has a van, you may need to reserve it. Or you may need to ask some of the

students' parents to see if they would be willing to transport the group. Be sure to check with your church office for policies regarding parental permission slips and legally authorized drivers. Also check with your minister about a medical release form for each student. Send a postcard to make the parents aware of the specifics of your trip.

Spend some time with your class explaining some of the things they may experience while you are visiting. For example: the unusual smell in a nursing home, people confined to wheelchairs and beds, people not responding to them because they cannot hear, etc. Have the students share with each other trips that they have made in the past to nursing homes or retirement centers. If no one has visited one before, ask what they think it will be like. Help the students understand how important it is for everyone to have visitors. You could have the students experiment with some of the challenges senior citizens sometimes face. For example, they could try to get around in a wheelchair. Put waxed paper on a pair of glasses and have them try to read a book. This activity can help to show what cataracts are like for older people. Tie one of their arms to their side and have them try to do ordinary tasks. Explain that this is what happens with a stroke sometimes. Use earplugs to demonstrate someone who is hard of hearing. It is important for students to recognize that many times the seniors have all their mental faculties but have physical limitations.

Tell the students that while they are at the center, they need to get the first and last name of at least one resident. After they return from the visit, they can send thank-you notes to the residents who talked with them.

Your class could sing some choruses that they enjoy for the residents. They could also say Bible verses that they have learned.

Help the children come up with questions that they could ask individual residents. The children may be more comfortable in pairs or by staying with the large group. Some questions may be: "In what year were you born? What was the most fun thing you did as a child? What was your favorite game? What are some of your family traditions?" The children may have questions of their own they would like to ask, too.

Before you leave the nursing home or retirement center, pray with the residents. If one of the children would like to pray, allow them to do this. If not, have one of the adults with your group close in prayer.

Allow time to debrief when you return to the church. Lead them in a discussion about their thoughts and reactions to the visit.

Winter—Adopt a Family

The holidays always bring stories of families in need. Encourage your class to adopt one or two families in your community who are in need.

Check your phone book for an agency that works with needy families. Explain to the agency that your class has been studying a unit on families. Tell the agency that the class would like to adopt one or two of these families for the holiday season. By adopting, explain that you will provide food, clothing, and Christmas gifts for adults and children. To accomplish this, ask the agency for clothing sizes from all members of the families.

Once you've received this information, help students organize their efforts. Have them divide into three committees, with each group working in one of the following areas.

1. Food Committee

Have these students plan the food collection. They could place marked boxes throughout the church building. Have a note printed in the church paper encouraging the congregation to donate nonperishable foods to the project. Be sure to set a deadline for the collection. If people would rather donate money, have them give it to the church office. (Make the church office aware of this ahead of time.) Then plan a shopping trip to buy the food needed. When all the food has been bought or collected, divide it evenly among the adopted families.

2. Clothing Committee

These students may want to set up their collection process in the same manner as the food committee. Have a note printed in the church paper listing the clothing sizes needed. Have a drop-off point and deadline set up for this activity too. Use cash donations in the same manner as the food committee, planning a shopping excursion if necessary. After the clothes are collected, sort through the items and separate them appropriately.

3. Gift Committee

These students will be in charge of collecting toys and other items to be used as Christmas gifts. If you do plan to do this activity, be sure to start this project well in advance of the holidays (one to two months).

Again, have church members donate new or slightly used toys to the project. After all the toys have been collected, set a time to wrap the gifts and get them ready for delivery.

When all the food, clothing, and gifts have been collected, wrapped, and organized, determine the delivery date and time. Check with the agency on how to best handle this. Some families might be embarrassed by charity. Having the agency deliver the gifts with a simple note that says, "Given in the name of Jesus by _____ Church," may be all the information that is needed. If permission to deliver the items has been granted, plan for a few students and at least one adult go to the homes. Keep the meeting simple by wishing the family Merry Christmas and inviting them to a service at your church. Be sensitive to the family's response. If they're not open to the invitation, be courteous and say good-bye. Your mission will have been accomplished.

Spring—Spruce Up the Neighborhood

This seasonal project will have students working to clean or fix homes of those in your congregation with a need. Acquire the names of elderly or fixed-income people in your church

Set a day for the students to perform odd jobs—painting, window washing, or yard work. You may want to divide the class into teams depending on the number of homes you have to visit. Make sure there is at least one adult supervisor for each team.

Once you have a list of the homes to visit and their needs, have students list the items they will need to bring—paint brushes, rags, cleaners, hoes, etc. Remind students that this is a service project so they should not accept any pay for their work.

This project is not only a great opportunity for service, but it's a wonderful way for students to become acquainted with others in their congregation they may not know.

Summer—Family Outreach Fair

This project could greatly benefit from the parent's involvement. Plan a day for a Free Family Fair. Have each individual family take responsibility for a booth at the fair. For example, one family could be in charge of a dunking booth, another the baked goods table, another the ring toss, and so forth. Set the fair up on the church grounds or parking lot. If your church is located in a sparsely populated neighborhood, consider having it in a city park.

Make sure the event is well publicized. Distribute fliers and send announcements to the local radio station. Do not give the impression that this is a profit-making event. Promote it as a day for families, by families, to have fun and enjoy each other's company.

Unit 3

Totally Cool Stuff Every Kid Should Know

An Introduction to the Basics of Church Life

Do you remember what it is like to be the new kid on the block? Perhaps you've been new to a job, a school, or a city. Whatever your situation, you probably experienced the trepidation and apprehension that comes with being a newcomer.

Imagine yourself as a newcomer to the church. You don't know where your class meets. You don't understand the lingo. You don't see anyone that you know. You feel insecure and awkward.

Now, imagine being ten years old and new to the church!

While the sessions in this unit will help ease the uncertainties of being new, several other factors are important as well. The success of making new kids feel like an important part of the church depends on people more than on lessons.

Teachers and classmates are keys to the newcomer's feelings of belonging. When a student doesn't feel liked or welcomed by either teachers or classmates, then he will not feel as if he belongs at church. As a teacher, it is important for you to engage in conversation with newcomers, to call them by name, to show genuine interest in them. Encourage students to be friendly with one another and discourage all name calling.

Following each session, give each student a photocopy of one note card from pages 89 or 90. Each card contains a week's worth of daily devotions that focus on the lesson topics.

These sessions also incorporate activities for other church members to present during the session time. When this is done, students will meet a variety of people from the church. Knowing people and seeing familiar, friendly faces around the building helps to foster a sense of belonging.

Knowing about the Bible is another key ingredient in helping a newcomer feel like a part of the church. That's where this unit will help. It is designed to introduce kids to four important topics discussed in the church. Through this orientation and through meeting the people of the church, new kids can feel at ease in the church setting.

Newcomers are not the only kids who can benefit from these sessions. Regular attendees will gain insight into church life through the study of this unit.

As a result of studying this unit, students will know basic information about four areas of church life. First, the Bible is God's message to them. Second, Jesus is the Christ, the Son of God. Third, salvation is found only in Jesus. Fourth, all people who follow Jesus (i.e. Christians) are the church.

Also as a result of studying this unit, students will desire to be a part of the church. Responding to their knowledge and desire, they will regularly attend events scheduled by their local church.

Key Verse—John 20:30, 31

These verses summarize this introduction to the church in that they tell us why the Bible was written—that you may believe that Jesus is the Christ, the Son of God. They state who Jesus is—the Christ, the Son of God. They tell us why believing in Jesus is important—life in His name. It communicates the heart of the message of the church—the message that every newcomer should know—Jesus.

Note Cards

Before each session, assemble a note card for each student. Photocopy the information provided on the next pages onto sturdy, colorful paper, then cut apart and fold like a note card. Give one card to each student and encourage him to complete one devotional activity each day. Following week one, mail note cards to absentees. Write a short, personal note to each student and remind him of the next meeting time.

Session 1

This session gives an overview of the Bible. Students will look at the unity, authority, and message of the Bible.

Know that the Bible is God's message to them.
Feel honored that God gave the Bible to them.
Present evidence that the Bible is God's message to them.

Session 2

This session focuses on Jesus. Students will look at who Jesus is, what Jesus did, and why Jesus came.

Know that Jesus is the Christ, God's Son.
Feel awed by Jesus.
Proclaim Jesus as the Christ, God's Son.

Session 3

This session focuses on how salvation works in the lives of those who have a relationship with Jesus. Students will look at how Jesus paid the penalty for sin, how He helps Christians with daily living, and how Jesus will free Christians from Satan forever.

Know that salvation is found only in Jesus.
Feel the desire for salvation.
Celebrate the gift of salvation.

Session 4

This session focuses on the importance of each person to the church. Many kids believe that while they need other church members, those church members don't need kids. Students will look at three ways the Bible describes the church: a body, a family, and a temple.

Know that all Christians together are called the church.
Feel important to and needed by the church.
Describe each person's importance to the church.

Session 1—Note Card Copy

The Bible is an amazing book. Find out more about it. Do one activity each day this week.

1. About forty (40) men wrote the books of the Bible. Among these men were a king, a prophet, a shepherd, a tax collector, and a doctor. Some books are named after the people who wrote them. Look in the Table of Contents in your Bible. What books were named after their writers?

2. The Bible has sixty-six (66) books that are divided into two Testaments: Old and New. Look in the Table of Contents of your Bible. How many books are part of the Old Testament? How many books are part of the New Testament?

3. Each Bible book is broken into chapters. Each chapter is broken into short sections called verses. All of the chapters and verses are numbered so it is easy to find your way around. A Bible reference is listed by book name, chapter number, and then verse number. The book and chapter number are listed at the top of each page. Chapter numbers are also listed in large print at the beginning of each chapter. Verse numbers are listed in small print at the beginning of each verse. Open your Bible to any page. Find the book name, a chapter number, and the verses.

4. The books of the Bible were written over fifteen hundred (1500) years. Genesis was the first book written. It tells about the beginning. Read the first verse in the Bible, Genesis 1:1. Revelation was the last book written. It tells about the end. Read the last verses in the Bible, Revelation 22:20, 21. (If you have trouble finding the book of Genesis or Revelation, look for the page number in the Table of Contents.)

5. Open your Bible to the middle. What book did you find? The book of Psalms is in the middle. The middle verses of the Bible are Psalm 117:1, 2. Find and read Psalm 117:1, 2. How has God shown His great love to you?

6. Bible scholars use the word *unity* to describe the Bible. The Bible has unity because it has 66 different books that were written by 40 different men over 1500 years, but all books tell about one God. Cool. All 66 books of the Bible work together to tell God's message to mankind. What is God's message to mankind? Find and read Luke 19:10 and John 20:30, 31.

7. The Bible is God's message to you. We have the Bible because God wants us to know Him and His Son Jesus. To know God and Jesus, we must read the Bible. Read 2 Timothy 3:15. Reading the Bible will tell you all you need to know about your salvation.

Session 3—Note Card Copy

Christians are people who follow and obey Jesus. Here are some things that the Bible tells Jesus' followers to do. These things help Christians have a good relationship with Jesus.

1. Christians have **faith.** Without faith it is impossible to please God. Read Hebrews 11:1, 6. Faith is believing in God even though you cannot see Him. Christians live by faith because they believe what God has told them in His word. Do you have faith in God?

2. Christians **repent.** They turn from sin to God. They stop doing wrong and start doing right. Read Acts 3:19. God wants everyone to repent. Read 2 Peter 3:9.

3. Christians **tell others** that Jesus is the Christ, the Son of God. Read Romans 10:9. Confession is telling. If we believe that Jesus is the Christ, the Son of God, we cannot keep it a secret.

4. Christians **pray.** Jesus taught His disciples how to pray. Read Matthew 6:1-13. This prayer tells Christians some important things for which to pray. What are they?

5. Christians **worship** God and Jesus because they want to tell them that they are special. When Christians thank Jesus for paying the penalty for sin, they worship Him. Worship God by reading Revelation 15:3, 4 aloud.

6. Christians remember Jesus when they take the **Lord's Supper.** Read 1 Corinthians 11:23-26. It is important that Christians remember that Jesus died for their sins. The special time that they remember this is during the Lord's Supper.

7. Christians look for **Jesus' return.** Read Acts 1:9, 10. When Jesus returns, Christians will be with the Lord forever. Jesus said that He is coming soon. He told His followers to watch and be ready.

 ©1996 by The Standard Publishing Company. Permission is granted to reproduce this page for ministry purposes only—not for resale.

Session 2—Note Card Copy

Find out more about Jesus by reading what He said about himself. Read one Scripture each day this week.

1. Jesus said, "I am the light of the world." Read John 8:12. Think about light. Why is light important? Light helps us to see in the dark. Why did Jesus call himself the "light of the world"? Jesus helps us see what is right and what is wrong. He helps us find our way to salvation.

2. Jesus said, "I am the gate (door)." Read John 10:9. Think about gates (doors). We enter places such as yards, houses, and rooms through gates (doors). Jesus called himself a gate because we can only enter Heaven through Him.

3. Jesus said, "I am the good shepherd." Read John 10:11. What does the good shepherd do for his sheep? He lays down his life for them. Jesus is a good shepherd because He laid down His life for you. He did this when He died on the cross for your sins.

4. Jesus said, "I am the way and the truth and the life." Read John 14:6. Jesus said this because He is the way to God. He is the truth about God. And He is the One who gives true life.

5. Jesus called himself a doctor for sinners. Read Luke 5:29-32. When we are feeling well, we don't need a doctor. We wait until we are sick to go see the doctor. Sinners are like sick people; they are sick with sin. Jesus is like a doctor because He helps sinners get well. He tells them to repent and follow Him.

6. Jesus called himself a servant. Read Mark 10:45. Jesus came to earth to serve us. He did that by paying the penalty for our sins. He died on the cross.

7. Jesus is risen! Read Mark 10:32-34. In these verses, Jesus describes what will happen to Him. These things happened just as Jesus said. Jesus did die, but He was resurrected. Jesus has power over death. He is alive!

Session 4—Note Card Copy

The book of Acts tells us about the beginning of the church. It tells us how the people worked together and used their talents to spread the good news about Jesus. Here are some ways the early church spread the gospel. Read one each day this week.

1. Peter preached a sermon. Read Acts 2:14, 22-24, 36-41. Peter told the people about Jesus' life, death, and resurrection. He told people that Jesus is Lord and Christ. He told them to repent and be baptized. The people listened and believed Peter. How many people were added to the church that day?

2. The believers worshiped together. Read Acts 2:44, 45. Everyday the believers met together in the temple courts. This helped the church grow. How often were new people becoming believers?

3. Peter and John helped the sick. Read Acts 3:1-10; 4:1-4. When Peter and John healed the crippled man, many people saw what happened. They wanted to know about the power that healed the man. Peter and John told them about Jesus. How many people believed in Jesus that day?

4. The believers shared their possessions. Read Acts 4:32-35. The early church took care of one another. They helped anyone who needed help. Some believers sold their property and used the money to help the poor. This helped the church grow.

5. Philip rode in a chariot. Read Acts 8:26-40. While Philip rode in the chariot, he told the Ethiopian about Jesus. What did the Ethiopian decide about Jesus?

6. Paul and Silas wouldn't escape from prison. Read Acts 16:22-34. When a violent earthquake freed Paul and Silas from prison, they chose to stay in prison. This saved the jailer's life, and the jailer asked Paul and Silas about Jesus. So Paul and Silas told the jailer and his family the good news about Jesus. What happened to the jailer and his family that night?

7. Peter raised Dorcas from the dead. Read Acts 9:36-43. Many people loved Dorcas because she helped them by making clothes for them. They were very sad when she died. Peter prayed and told Dorcas to "get up." She did. Many people believed in the Lord.

90   ©1996 by The Standard Publishing Company. Permission is granted to reproduce this page for ministry purposes only—not for resale.

Session 1

Cool Stuff About the Bible

Scripture. 2 Peter 1:16-21; 2 Timothy 3:16, 17; John 20:30, 31

Know that the Bible is God's message to them.

Feel honored that God gave the Bible to them.

Present evidence that the Bible is God's message to them.

Get Into the Game

Make sure each student has a Bible to use during today's session. Before class, prepare three strips of poster board. Write these words on separate strips: unity, authority, message.

"The Bible is an important book. It has been translated into more than 2000 languages. The printing press was invented so that copies of the Bible could be made faster. The Bible is the best selling book in the world. It is the most famous book of all time.

"Why is the Bible so famous and important? Other religions in the world today believe that their special books are just as or more important than the Bible. Yet, none of those books compare with the Bible. We believe that the Bible is the Word of God. How do we know that the Bible is the Word of God?"

Have students discuss why they think they know the Bible is God's Word. List their answers on the chalkboard.

"The Bible is a very important book to Christians. Today we're going to discover three reasons why the Bible is the most important book in the world. We know the Bible is God's Word because of its unity, authority, and message."

Show poster board cards at the appropriate time.

Materials
Bibles, poster board cut into three strips

Step 1

"We will work in small groups to discover why we can believe that the Bible is the Word of God. One group will explore the Bible's unity. Another group will look at the Bible's authority. The third group will discover the Bible's message."

Divide students into three groups to do the following activities. Have an adult available for each group to guide the activity. Each smaller group will report back to the large group concerning the content of their activity.

Activity #1—On the Trail (Unity)

Distribute "On the Trail" and have students complete it. Use the comments below to discuss the Bible's unity.

"The Bible was written by forty men over fifteen hundred years. This means that the writers did not work together to decide what to write. Many of them were not alive at the same time. Yet they all wrote about one God and told His story of how He sent His Son Jesus to earth.

"Bible scholars use the word *unity* to describe the Bible. The Bible has unity because it has 66 different books that were written by 40 different men over 1500 years, but all books tell about one God. Cool. All 66 books of the Bible work together to tell God's message to mankind. What is God's message to mankind?"

Find and read Luke 19:10 and John 20:30, 31.

"We have the Bible because God wants us to know Him and His Son Jesus. Cool."

When page 95 and the discussion are finished, students will make a secret message paper for each student in class today. Some of the unity facts will need to be repeated. To make the secret messages, students will dip a cotton swab into the lemon juice and write the message on white paper. The lemon juice will dry clear.

Heating the message papers with a heated iron or holding them up to a hot light bulb will reveal the message.

Materials
photocopies of page 95 for each student, pencils, lemon juice squeezed into bowls, cotton swabs, white paper, an iron or access to a hot light bulb

Activity #2—Press Conference (Authority)

Photocopy the script "Writers of the Bible" for you and each student. Provide Bible-times costumes. Guide the group to prepare the skit to perform for the rest of the class. This script is written for a cast of eight. For four students eliminate the parts of Ezekiel, Moses, and Peter. Combine the parts of the Mediator and the Reporter.

Materials
photocopies of pages 96, 97, Bible-times costumes, lectern or podium

Activity #3—Got the Message? (Message)

Assign these Scriptures to be read aloud in the order that follows.

Have students read through their assigned verses several times so that they will read them with fluency and expression.

Then have students work together to form each letter of the word *salvation* with their bodies. They can stand or lie on the floor to form the letters.

For their presentation, this group will follow the script. Have the group practice the parts they say in unison.

Materials
Bibles for each student

Got the Message? Cool.

All in unison: What's God's message in the Bible?

Read Isaiah 53:6.
Read Romans 3:23.
Read Romans 6:23.
Read Matthew 1:21.
Read Luke 19:10.
Read John 3:16.
Read Acts 4:12.
Read 1 Thessalonians 5:10.
Read Acts 2:21

All in unison: God's message is (students spell out letters in the word salvation, shouting each letter when it is formed) S-A-L-V-A-T-I-O-N! Got the message? Salvation! Cool!

Step 2

Each group discovered more information about three reasons—unity, authority, message—why the Bible is the most important book in the world. (Show poster board words as each reason is introduced.)

Group 1 will tell us more about the Bible's unity. (Group 1 presents.) Group 2 will tell us about the Bible's authority. (Group 2 presents their press conference.) Group 3 will tell us more about the message of the Bible. (Group 3 presents.)

These things—unity, authority, and salvation message—set the Bible apart from any other book in the world. No other book can claim its unity of purpose, its authority of God, and its salvation message of the Bible. These reasons give us confidence that the Bible is truly the Word of God.

Step 3

Before class ask three adults to tell how using the Bible has influenced their lives. Ask them to share from one of these perspectives: the Bible as a guidebook that shows us how to live, the Bible as God's book of revelation that teaches about God and Jesus, the Bible as an answer book for questions that people ask: Where did we come from? Why is there evil in the world? What does the future hold? and so on. Each guest should emphasize that the Bible is a book to be read.

"The Bible is an important book because it is the Word of God. It is God's message to us. The Bible was given to us by God for a purpose. God wants us to read and study the Bible. When we read and study the Bible, we will know God. We can find salvation, and we will know how to live our lives. Knowing that the Bible is God's message to us should make us want to read and study it.

"We have some guests with us today that are going to tell

Materials
three adults to tell about the Bible's influence in their lives

how reading and studying the Bible has changed their lives." When adults are finished, have students tell how the Bible has helped them. Be sure to share yourself.

Take It to the Next Level

Divide the class into the three groups they were in for Step 1. Instruct each group to create a commercial or slogan to "advertise" the Bible. They are to use facts presented during today's lesson to prove that the Bible is the Word of God, how it is useful to them, and that it should be read and studied by them. Walk among the groups and help them as needed. Allow them to make notes or use the poster board for cue cards. If students have trouble, suggest that they adapt a commercial from television. Help assure that their content is correct.

Some examples that might be helpful: "Life is short; pray hard. Read the Bible—Just do it!" (Nike), "The Bible—try it again for the first time!" (cornflakes).

Ask the students to present their commercials. If you have access to video equipment, record the commercials.

"The Bible is God's Word. We know the Bible is God's Word because of its unity. It was written by 40 men over 1500 years, and it tells mankind God's message of salvation.

"We know the Bible is God's Word because it has God's authority. Old Testament writers told us more than 2500 times that the Bible is God's message. New Testament writers were eyewitnesses to Jesus' life. They also told us how God's authority is on every page of the Bible.

"We know the Bible is God's Word because of its message of salvation. The Bible is the only book that tells us that people need salvation. The message of God is a message of salvation.

"We can be certain that the Bible is God's Word. The Bible can't do us any good unless we use it. We must read it and study it so that we can know God and His message of salvation. John 20:30, 31 says, 'Jesus did many other miraculous signs in the presence of his disciples, which are not recorded in this book. But these are written that you may believe that Jesus is the Christ, the Son of God, and that by believing you may have life in his name.'

"I feel honored that God has given His message to me. Do you feel honored too? If we feel honored, then we should respond by reading and studying God's Word." Distribute the devotional cards for this week from page 89. "Here is a guide that will help you read and study the Bible. Follow it each day. Let's respond now by committing ourselves to study God's Word. We'll do so with a moment of silent prayer followed by my closing prayer."

Materials
paper, pens, poster board, markers, video recording equipment (optional)

On the Trail

The Bible is a pretty "cool" book. Its unity is one reason why. Follow each path to discover facts about the Bible's unity.

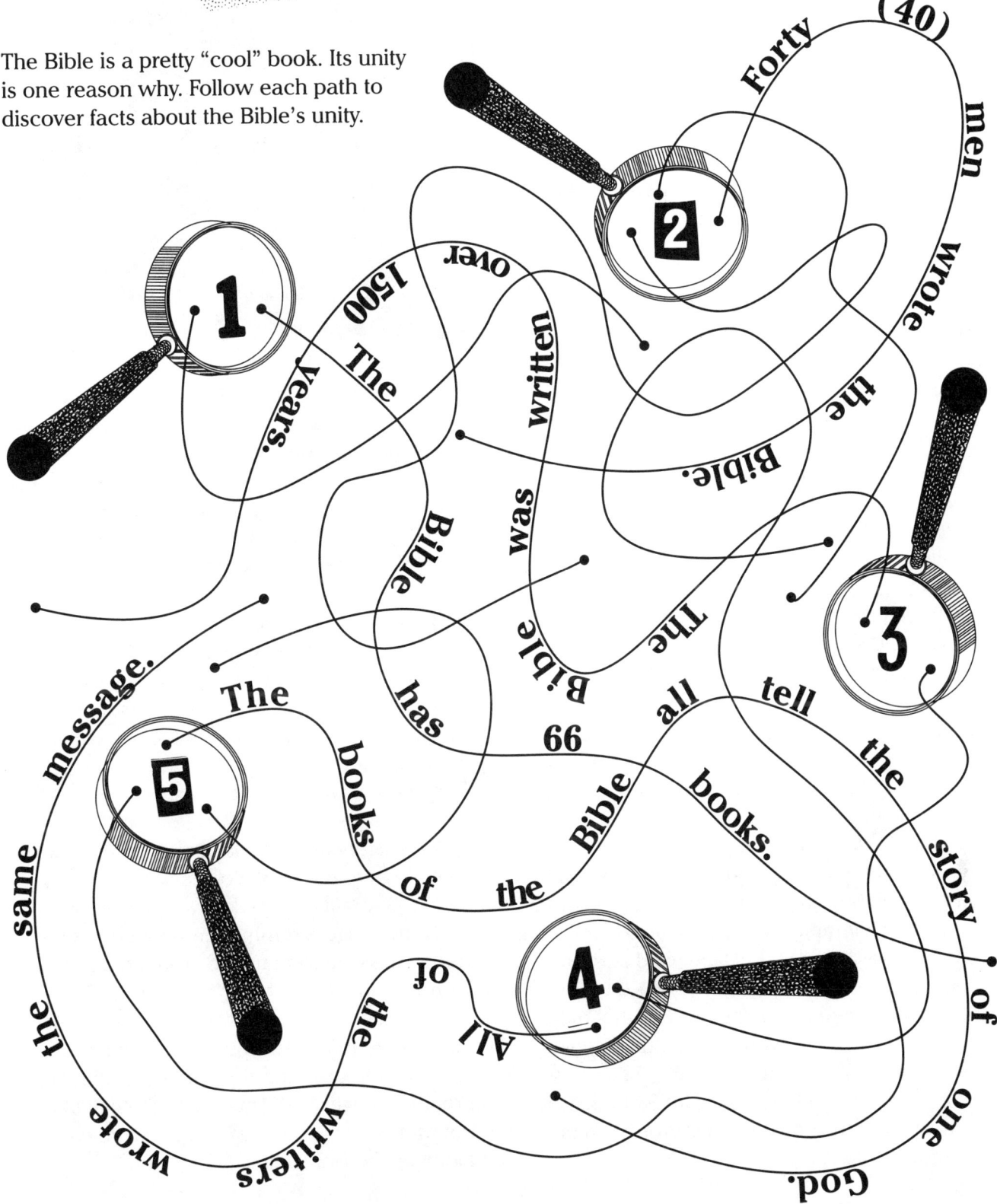

©1996 by The Standard Publishing Company. Permission is granted to reproduce this page for ministry purposes only—not for resale.

Writers of the Bible
Press Conference

(Set a stage area with seven chairs and a lectern or podium. The six Bible writers and the mediator should sit in the chairs.)

Mediator *(stands behind lectern):* Welcome. Today, we hope to unlock the mystery of how 40 writers over a period of 1500 years wrote 66 books about one God and His plan for mankind. With us today are Matthew, a tax collector; Samuel, Ezekiel, and Moses, prophets; Peter, a fisherman; and Paul, a missionary. *(Writers stand as their names are mentioned.)* We'll have a statement from each writer, and then we will open for questions.

Moses *(stands behind lectern):* I'm Moses, a prophet of God. I wrote the first five books of the Bible: Genesis, Exodus, Leviticus, Numbers, and Deuteronomy. When I wrote, I used these words, "The Lord said to Moses," so that you would know the words in my books were from God. Many Old Testament writers used a phrase like this to tell us their words were from God.

Samuel *(stands behind lectern):* I'm Samuel. My story is written in 1 and 2 Samuel. When I was a small boy, my mother, Hannah, took me to live at the temple. I grew up learning to listen to God. I was a prophet of God. God told me what to say, and I said it. In my books, I wrote that I spoke the word of the Lord so that those who read my books would know that I spoke the message of God. In 1 Samuel 3:19, I wrote these words: "The Lord was with Samuel as he grew up, and he let none of his words fall to the ground."

Ezekiel *(stands behind lectern):* I'm Ezekiel, the writer of the book Ezekiel. I was God's prophet who cried out God's warnings to His people. In my book, I wrote "the hand of the Lord was upon me" so that those who read my book would know that I spoke the message of God. I also said, "The word of the Lord came to me."

Matthew *(stands behind lectern):* I'm the apostle Matthew, the writer of the New Testament book Matthew. I was an eyewitness to the events I wrote in my book. I saw and heard what Jesus said and did. I was with Jesus many times when He quoted the Old Testament as the Word of God.

Peter *(stands behind lectern):* I'm the apostle Peter. I wrote the books of 1 and 2 Peter. I warn believers about those who would lie about God's message. I remind them that the Bible is God's message to mankind. The Bible is a trustworthy guide. Its authors "spoke from God." In 2 Peter 1:20, 21, I wrote, "Above all, you must understand that no prophecy of Scripture came about by the prophet's own interpretation. For prophecy never had its origin in the will of man, but men spoke from God as they were carried along by the Holy Spirit."

96 ©1996 by The Standard Publishing Company. Permission is granted to reproduce this page for ministry purposes only—not for resale.

Paul *(stands behind lectern):* I'm the apostle Paul. I wrote several of the New Testament letters. In 2 Timothy 3:16, 17, I tell about the importance of God's Word. "All scripture is God-breathed and is useful for teaching, rebuking, correcting and training in righteousness, so that the man of God may be thoroughly equipped for every good work." Only the Word of God does what it says it will do. That's because it is God's message.

Mediator *(at lectern):* Thank you, writers. Now we will take questions.

Reporter *(stands in place):* Moses, you said that many Old Testament writers used a phrase like, "the Lord said to me," to let people know that the writer was speaking God's Word. How often does this happen in the Old Testament?

Moses: Phrases that give God the credit for the message of the Bible occur over 2500 times. It is important for us to know that Bible writers didn't make up what they wrote. They wrote the message of God, and they wrote it with God's authority.

Reporter *(stands):* Samuel, how do we know that the writers of the Bible were writing the message of God?

Samuel: The Bible claims to be the direct message or revelation of God. There are many books that people believe to be as special as the Bible. Yet, these books do not claim to be the direct revelation of God. The Bible writers believed they were writing the message of God because they told us with phrases such as, "the Lord says." These words give the Bible God's authority—something no other book has.

Reporter *(stands):* Ezekiel, will you explain why God's authority over the Bible is important?

Ezekiel: God's authority over the Bible tells us where the Bible came from. It came from God. It is God's message to us. Because the Bible has God's authority, we can trust it completely as the Word of God. If the Bible didn't have God's authority, it would be no different from any other book that gives good moral advice.

Reporter *(stands):* Matthew, tell us about one time that Jesus showed He believed the Old Testament to be the Word of God.

Matthew: Jesus often quoted Old Testament Scriptures. He taught from the Scriptures. Jesus called the Old Testament *God's Word* when He asked, "Have you not read what God said to you?" (Matthew 22:31).

Reporter *(stands):* Peter, how can we be sure that the writers of the Bible didn't make up the things they wrote and then say that their words were from God?

Peter: Deuteronomy 18:22 gives us the answer, "If what a prophet proclaims in the name of the Lord does not take place or come true, that is a message that the Lord has not spoken." We know that all the prophecies written about Jesus were fulfilled. The Bible tells us about more things that will happen. We know these things will happen too. Another fact—40 writers wrote the Bible over 1500 years—proves that the Bible is God's Word. These writers could not deliver an identical message—God's message—without God's authority. We can be sure that the Bible is God's Word.

Reporter *(stands):* Paul, we've heard several of you tell us that the Bible is God's message to mankind. What is that message?

Paul: The Bible message is a message of salvation. The Old Testament tells us how God prepared people for the birth and life of His Son, Jesus. The New Testament tells us how Jesus brought us salvation. John 20:31 tells us why the Bible was written, so "that you may believe that Jesus is the Christ, the Son of God, and that by believing you may have life in his name." The Bible really is God's message of salvation.

end

97 ©1996 by The Standard Publishing Company. Permission is granted to reproduce this page for ministry purposes only—not for resale.

Session 2

Cool Stuff About Jesus

Scripture. Acts 2:22-24; John 20:30, 31

Know that Jesus is the Christ, the Son of God.
Feel awed by Jesus.
Proclaim Jesus as the Christ, the Son of God.

Get Into the Game

Begin the session with the following chant. If possible have several adults perform it in unison. "There's one name that's above every name. It's Jesus (clap, clap). Jesus (clap, clap)." Repeat several times and ask students to join in. Finish with a strong "Jesus" followed by no claps. Then sing the song, "Jesus, Name Above All Names," by Naida Hearn. Discuss the lyrics with the following questions.

How do we know Jesus' name is more important than any other name? (Jesus' name is a name above all names.) What are the other names for Jesus? (Savior, Lord, Emmanuel, Redeemer, Word) What does the name Emmanuel mean? (God is with us) What words describe His names? (beautiful, glorious, blessed, living)

"Why is Jesus is so important that people praise Him by saying that His name is above all names?" Discuss. "Jesus' name is important because of who He is (beautiful Savior, glorious Lord), what He did (be with us), and why He came (blessed Redeemer)."

Step 1

"We will work in small groups. Each group will explore one reason why Jesus' name is the most important name in the world. One group will look at who Jesus is. One will explore what Jesus did. The third will discover why Jesus came." Explain the following activities. Then divide students into three groups, one group for each activity. Have an adult available to guide each group. "When our groups are finished, we will report what we learned to the entire group."

*Activity #1—*Cool Names (Who Jesus Is)

Students will make a colorful backdrop that displays some of

Jesus means *Savior* or *Yahweh saves.* Jesus is our Savior because He died to save us from our sins.
Christ means anointed one. It tells that Jesus was chosen by God to die for man's sins.
Lord is a title of respect telling of Jesus' authority.
Master is a title of respect used by Jesus' followers.
Messiah is the Hebrew word for the *anointed one* whom God sent to establish His kingdom on earth.
Prophets are authorized to speak the word of God to man. Jesus was sent by God to speak God's message. Jesus brought God's message of salvation.
Shepherd. Jesus is the good shepherd who lays down His life for his sheep. Jesus laid down His life for us when He died on the cross.
Immanuel means *God is with us.* It reminds us that Jesus is God.
Redeemer. Jesus is our redeemer because His death and resurrection redeemed, or saved, us from our sins.
Word. John calls Jesus the Word. Jesus was with God before He came to earth. Jesus came to show us and tell us about God.
Son of God is a title that reminds us that Jesus has a unique relationship to God. Jesus is God's Son.
Lamb is a title that reveals that Jesus was the perfect sacrifice given in payment for our sins.

the names and titles of Jesus. Provide colorful art paper (cut each sheet into fourths), scissors, pinking sheers, paper clips, glue, cellophane tape, and string.

Have students find and read Acts 2:22-24.

"Jesus' miracles prove that He was sent by God. Jesus' death and resurrection prove that He was sent by God. Jesus' names and titles also help us know that Jesus is the Son of God. Jesus has many names and titles. Each one is important because each one tells us something about Jesus. These names and titles help us know that Jesus is God's Son. They help us know that Jesus was sent by God. What are some of Jesus' names or titles?" Discuss, then read the list of names below.

"Our group will make accordion names using these names and titles of Jesus." Let students choose one name or title. Students need to select two art paper sections for each letter of their assigned name or title, one for the base and one for the letter. Students will draw each letter of the word either free-hand or with stencils. They will paste each letter to a base section of paper and decorate it with cuts of paper. Caution students not to disguise the letters when they decorate them. When finished decorating, lay the letters in order, vertically. Use clear cellophane tape to attach the sections together. Fold the sections of each name accordion style. Loosely attach a paper clip to the edge, not the bottom, of each word. Attach a piece of string to the paper clip.

Attach the folded papers to the wall with masking tape. Make sure only the top letter is attached. Also, make sure the accordion folded papers are high enough on the wall to display all the letters of each word when they are unfolded. To reveal the word, students pull on the string, removing the paper clip, and the accordion names will unfold.

Students may choose from the names and titles listed in the column for the accordion name folds. Also have them prepare to read the description with each name or title. At the appropriate time in the lesson, each student will read the name, pull the paper clip to unfold the name, and then read the description.

Activity #2—Miracles, Wonders, Signs (What Jesus Did)
The purpose of this activity is to discover miracles, wonders, and signs that affirm Jesus' identity.

Students will prepare a rebus game with some miracles, wonders, and signs concerning Jesus.

Have students find and read Acts 2:22-24 and John 3:2; 9:1-3, 32, 33; 20:30, 31. If students are familiar with miracles, wonders, and signs from Jesus' life, have them make a list. If not, have them choose from the lists given below.

Materials
Bibles, colorful art paper, scissors, pinking shears, paper clips, glue, cellophane tape, string

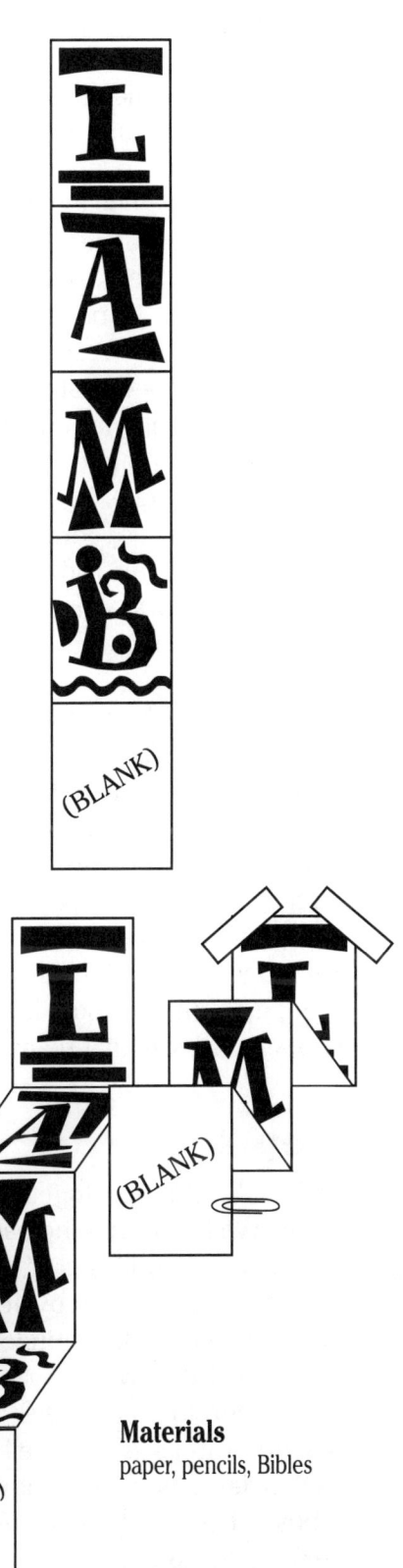

Materials
paper, pencils, Bibles

Read and discuss each event. Work together to write a brief sentence to describe each event. Then discuss how students could draw a rebus of each sentence. A rebus combines pictures and letters to form a sentence. Have students write out each rebus to copy from during their presentation time. During their presentation, this group will draw each rebus on the chalkboard for the rest of the class to decipher. A rebus example follows: (picture of fire) - re + (picture of a vest) -st x 1000 + (picture of map legend showing east) -s + (picture of a fish). The answer is: 5000 eat fish.

Miracles: Jesus feeds 5000 (Matthew 14:15-21); Jesus walks on water (Matthew 14:22-27); Jesus heals ten men with leprosy (Luke 17:1-19); Jesus raises Lazarus from the dead (John 11:38-44); Jesus is resurrected (Luke 24:1-6).

Wonders: Jesus walks unharmed through an angry crowd that wants to kill him (Mark 4:28); Jesus is transformed and meets with Elijah and Moses (Matthew 17:1-3); Jesus is taken into Heaven (Acts 1:9, 10).

Signs: A star appeared when Jesus was born (Matthew 2:1, 2); God said, "This is my Son" (Matthew 3:16, 17); darkness covered the earth when Jesus died (Matthew 27:45); the curtain in the temple tore when Jesus died (Matthew 27:50, 51).

Activity #3—**The Bureau of Lost and Found (Why Jesus Came)**

Make copies of the skit for your students and yourself. Set the stage using one table with three telephones and a very large book. Three bureau agents are to sit at the tables, each with his own phone, paper pad, and pen. All three agents pretend to talk on the phones, taking phone call after phone call. Each one will be highlighted in one part of the skit.

Set up a phone booth about ten feet from the table with one phone and a sign that reads, "Bureau of Lost and Found Hotline."

Step 2

Call all the students together. "Today we are learning about Jesus. We know that the name of Jesus is the most important name in the world. Jesus' name is above every name. Each one of our groups discovered some pretty cool things about Jesus that will help us understand why Jesus is so important.

"Group 1 discovered who Jesus is. (Have Group 1 present their accordion names.) Group 2 discovered some miracles, wonders, and signs that tell us what Jesus did and that show us that Jesus was sent from God. (Have Group 2 present their rebuses.) Group 3 discovered why Jesus came. (Have Group 3 perform the skit.)

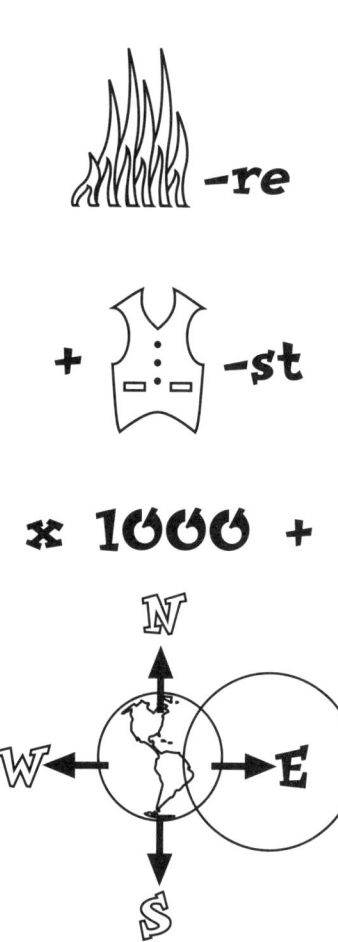

Materials
four telephones, three pads of paper, three pencils, a large book, a poster board sign that reads "Bureau of Lost and Found Hotline," table, chairs, photocopies of page 103

"These things about Jesus—who Jesus is, what Jesus did, and why Jesus came—help us understand that Jesus was a very special man. These things help us understand why Jesus' name is holy. We honor Jesus' name because of who He is—the Son of God. We honor Jesus' name because of His miracles, wonders, and signs. We honor Jesus' name because He came to save us from our sins."

Step 3

"The reason that Jesus came is the most important reason why we honor Jesus' name. We honor Jesus for coming to earth to save us because He suffered so much for us. We honor Him because He died on a cross for our sins and because He conquered death when He was resurrected. Today, He lives in Heaven with God."

Option 1: Ask an adult Sunday school class to act out the events surrounding the death and resurrection of Jesus.

Option 2: Direct students to read through the accounts of Jesus' death, burial, and resurrection. Before class, gather pictures that show the events in the last week of Jesus' life.

1. God sent Jesus to save us from our sins (Matthew 1:20, 21).
2. Jesus was arrested (Mark 14:43-46).
3. "Crucify him" (Mark 15:1-5).
4. Jesus was nailed to a cross (Mark 15:21-32).
5. Jesus died and darkness covered the land (Mark 15:33-38).
6. Jesus was buried in a tomb (Mark 15:42-47).
7. Jesus rose from the dead (Mark 16:1-8).
8. Jesus appeared to many people after His resurrection (Mark 16:9-14).
9. Jesus returned to Heaven (Acts 1:9, 10).
10. Jesus died for me (John 3:16)!

"Jesus came to earth to die for the sins of all mankind. He died because of my sins. He died because of your sins. He died for us so that we could have a relationship with God. Without Jesus, we cannot find our way to God." Have students find and read John 14:6. "Jesus said that He is the way to God; He is the truth about God; He is the way to eternal life with God. Jesus' name is so honored and important because it is the name by which we are saved."

Have students find and read Acts 2:21 and Acts 4:12.

Take It to the Next Level

Students will make T-shirts or posters that proclaim Jesus as God's Son. Provide plenty of work space and protect it with newspaper. Provide a white T-shirt or poster board for each

Materials
an adult Sunday school class to perform the events surrounding the death of Jesus, or pictures showing events from the last week of Jesus' life, Bibles

Materials
white T-shirts or poster board panels for each student, fabric paint, photocopies of pages 90 and 104, paper, black markers

student, fabric paints of various colors, and copies of page 104. Shirts may need to be laundered before applying the fabric paint. See paint label. If providing T-shirts is not feasible, provide poster board and have students make posters.

The reproducible page should be placed inside the shirt and traced over using the fabric paint. If the design is difficult to see through the T-shirt, have students attach the shirt to a sunny window by placing wide tape around the top and sides, leaving the bottom open. The back lighting will make the pattern easier to see. Students may add other decorations to their shirts. Once students have completed their T-shirts, allow them to dry according to the fabric paint's recommendations.

Students may use the pattern from the reproducible page for their T-shirt design or create their own. If students create their own slogans, guide them to brainstorm ideas. Encourage students to recall what was discussed today when creating slogans. Write all the ideas on the chalkboard or poster board. If students choose to create their own shirts, provide paper and black markers. Have them work out their designs on the paper before applying them to the shirts. Then students may trace over their designs by placing the papers inside the shirt.

When the students have finished, ask them to show and read their messages.

"We know that Jesus is the Son of God because of the many names and titles He has. Each name and title tells us something important about Jesus.

"We also know that Jesus is the Son of God because of the many proofs we have in miracles, wonders, and sign. Jesus did these miraculous things so that we would believe He is God's Son. We know that Jesus is God's Son because He told us why He came: to save the lost.

"We know that Jesus is the Son of God because of His death and resurrection. Only Jesus, who lived a perfect life, could die for man's sins. Only Jesus, who had power over death, could be raised back to life after being dead.

"Jesus had an awesome life. John tells us why Jesus' awesome life is important to you and me. John 20:30, 31 says, 'Jesus did many other miraculous things in the presence of his disciples, which are not recorded in this book. But these are written that you may believe that Jesus is the Christ, the Son of God and that by believing you may have life in his name.'

"We made our T-shirts today so that we could be reminded about the awesome life of Jesus. When we wear them, we will proclaim that Jesus is the Son of God."

Close with prayer. Distribute and encourage students to continue following the devotion cards (page 90).

The Bureau of Lost and Found

(Sally walks up to phone booth and reads the sign. She enters the booth and picks up phone. It automatically dials. Phone rings.)

Agent Wright: Hello, this is the Bureau of Lost and Found, Agent Wright speaking. How may I help you?

Sally: Hello. My name is Sally, and I'm lost.

Wright: Hello, Sally. You've made a wise choice to call the Bureau of Lost and Found. Our Bureau has been here for over 1900 years helping lost people like you.

Sally: Well, I'm lost. I know I'm lost, but I don't know how to find my way. That's why I called. I don't know the way.

Wright: Jesus said, "I am the way, the truth and the life. No one comes to the father except through me." Sally, you are lost, but Jesus is the way. Jesus came to earth to seek and to save those who are lost. He came to save you.

Sally: Thank you Agent Wright. Good-bye.

Wright: Good-bye, Sally.

(Sally exits phone booth and almost bumps into Charlie, who has been studying the sign. Charlie enters the booth and picks up the phone. It automatically dials. Phone rings.)

Agent Meadows: Hello, Bureau of Lost and Found, Agent Meadows speaking. How may I help you?

Charlie: Hello, my name is Charlie. My sister and I had a fight. She says I'm lost and that she is found. Will you check and let me know?

Meadows: Please hold one moment Charlie while I check the Book of Life. *(Meadows lays down phone, reaches for the book and begins to flip through the pages, stops on a page, sighs and murmurs, "Interesting," then returns to the phone.)* Charlie, your sister appears to be right. Her name is listed in the Book. Your name is missing from the book.

Charlie: So I am lost.

Meadows: Charlie, the Book of Life lists every name of every person who has been given the gift of salvation. We are told in Acts 4:12 that

salvation is found only in Jesus. Luke 19:10 tells us that Jesus came to seek and to save the lost. Charlie, you don't have to stay lost. You can claim Jesus as your Lord and Savior.

Charlie: Thank you Agent Meadows. Good-bye.

Meadows: Good-bye, Charlie.

(Charlie exits the booth. Carlos walks up to him.)

Carlos: Excuse me. Can you tell me where I am? I think I'm lost.

Charlie: This is the corner of Wilshire and Newton. *(Charlie points to the sign on the phone booth.)*

Carlos: Thanks. *(Hurries into booth and picks up the phone. It automatically dials. Phone rings.)*

Agent Harlow: Hello, Bureau of Lost and Found, Agent Harlow speaking. How may I help you?

Carlos: Hi, I'm Carlos. I am curious about your bureau. Just exactly what do you do?

Harlow: The Bureau's only job is to help people who are lost.

Carlos: Good, because I'm lost. I'm at the corner of Wilshire and Newton. I need to find my way to Hamilton Avenue.

Harlow: Our bureau's job is to help people who are lost because they are without Jesus. Carlos, do you know Jesus?

Carlos: No. I only know that I'm at the corner of Wilshire and Newton and I should be on Hamilton.

Harlow: Carlos, Jesus is the Son of God. God sent Jesus to earth to save lost people. While Jesus was here, He performed miracles, wonders, and signs so that we would believe that He is God's Son and so that we could trust Him to save us.

Carlos: So I am lost without Jesus. Even if I was on Hamilton Avenue, I'd still be lost.

Harlow: That is true, Carlos.

Carlos: Thank you agent Harlow. Good-bye.

Harlow: Good-bye, Carlos.

103 ©1996 by The Standard Publishing Company. Permission is granted to reproduce this page for ministry purposes only—not for resale.

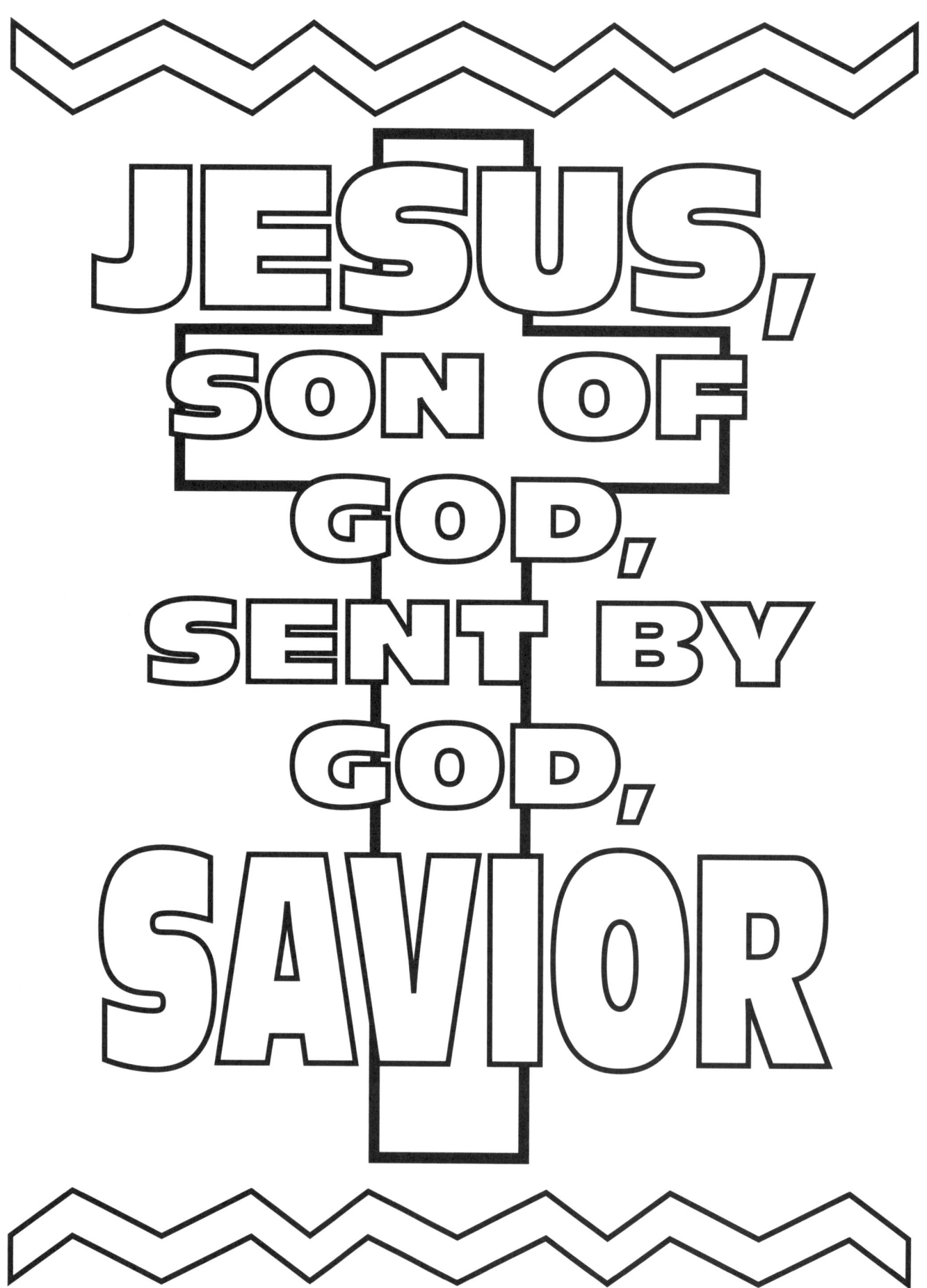

JESUS, SON OF GOD, SENT BY GOD, SAVIOR

 ©1996 by The Standard Publishing Company. Permission is granted to reproduce this page for ministry purposes only—not for resale.

Cool Stuff About Being a Christian

Scripture. Acts 4:12; Philippians 1:6; John 20:30, 31

Know that salvation is found only through Jesus.
Feel the desire for salvation.
Celebrate the gift of salvation.

Get Into the Game

Before class, write the letters in the words *believers* and *Christians* on separate sheets of paper. Place the letter side to the wall and tape them in place in front of your meeting area. When students gather, ask for two volunteers to participate in the game. Tell them that both of the words are names for the same group of people. Have players alternate turns asking for letters. When a player guesses a letter, turn it over. Continue until all letters of both words are facing forward.

"These words describe people who follow Jesus. Followers of Jesus were first called believers. Later they were called Christians." Read Acts 2:44; 11:26. A Christian is a person who has a personal relationship with Jesus Christ. The word Christian means belonging to Christ. Christians follow and obey Jesus.

"Being a Christian——having a personal relationship with Jesus—is the most important relationship a person can have. Why do you think that having a personal relationship with Jesus is important?" Have students respond.

Have students find and read Acts 4:12. "Salvation is found only in Jesus. Jesus paid the penalty for mankind's sin. Because Jesus died on the cross, we can be saved. Today, we are going to look at some cool things that Jesus does for Christians—those who have a personal relationship with Him."

Materials
drawing paper, pens or markers, tape

Step 1

Before class, make one copy of "Paying the Price" for each student. Separate the strips. Give the appropriate tokens to each group to prepare.

Materials
photocopies of page 110, markers, scissors, paper, glue, blanket, string

105

In class, have pupils find and read Philippians 1:6.

"This verse tells us three things that God does for Christians through Jesus. First, God begins a good work in Christians. Then He carries on that work. Third, He will complete His work. We will divide into three groups to discover what these three gifts are that Jesus gives to Christians."

Divide the students into three groups, one group for each activity. Have an adult available to guide each activity.

Activity #1—He Began a Good Work (Forgiveness)

Direct students to decorate an area or create an obstacle for each of the following stops. They should label each stop with the stop number and the title of the stop. Students will copy the sign information for each stop on a piece of paper and post it at each stop. Students will also prepare the "My penalty's paid" tokens.

Sign 1: You are a sinner. The penalty for sin is death. "For all have sinned and fall short of the glory of God" (Romans 3:23). "For the wages of sin is death" (Romans 6:23). Suggestion: Drape a blanket over several chairs. Students must crawl inside to read the sign.

Sign 2. You meet Jesus. You know that you can accept Jesus' payment. He paid the penalty for your sins. Suggestion: Make a paper cross and attach it to the wall or use a ready-made cross.

Sign 3: You accept Jesus' gift. God begins His work in you with forgiveness. You are freed from the penalty for sin and baptized. Take a "My penalty's paid!" token. Your sins have been forgiven on account of His name (1 John 2:12). Suggestion: Put this stop in the hallway outside the room. Place the "My penalty's paid" tokens here.

Activity #2—He Will Carry It On (Help in Daily Living)

Pupils will discover that Jesus helps Christians by providing a way out in times of temptation. Pupils will make three stops of a nine-stop course. Provide markers, paper, scissors, glue, and the "I have power over sin" tokens.

Direct students to decorate an area or create an obstacle for each of the following stops. They should label each stop with the stop number and the title of the stop. Students will copy the sign information for each stop on a piece of paper and post it at each stop. Students will also prepare the "I have power over sin" tokens.

Sign 4: Satan continues to tempt you to sin. "Each one is tempted when, by his own evil desire, he is dragged away and enticed" (James 1:14). Suggestion: If weather permits, send students outside to a tree. If not, place the stop near a window with a view of a tree.

Materials

markers, scissors, paper, glue, "My penalty's paid" tokens

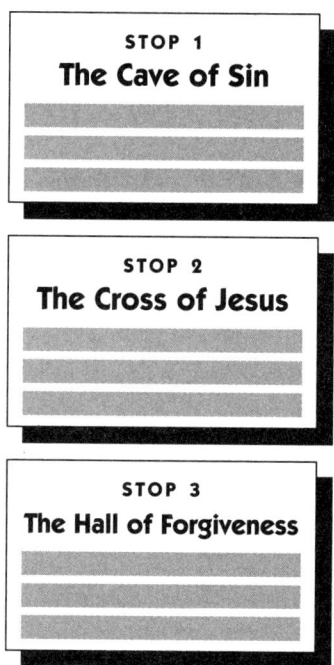

Materials

markers, paper, scissors, glue, "I have power over sin" tokens

Sign 5: Jesus provides a way out every time you are tempted. "God is faithful; he will not let you be tempted beyond what you can bear. But when you are tempted, he will also provide a way out so that you can stand up under it" (1 Corinthians 10:13). Suggestion: Use a doorway.

Sign 6: God continues His work in you. He gives you power over sin. Take an "I have power over sin" token. "Because he himself suffered when he was tempted, he is able to help those who are being tempted" (Hebrews 2:18). Suggestion: Make a paper road. Place the "I have power over sin" tokens here.

Activity #3—He Will Complete It (Eternal Life)

Pupils will discover that when Jesus returns, Christians will be freed from Satan's power. Pupils will make three stops of a nine-stop course. Provide markers, paper, scissors, glue, and the "I'm through with Satan" tokens.

Direct students to decorate an area or create an obstacle for each of the following stops. They should label each stop with the stop number and the title of the stop. Students will copy the sign information for each stop on a piece of paper and post it at each stop. Students will also prepare the "I'm through with Satan" tokens.

Materials

markers, paper, scissors, glue, "I'm through with Satan" tokens

Sign 7: You continue to battle Satan. "For our struggle is not against flesh and blood, but against the rulers, against the authorities, against the powers of this dark world and against the spiritual forces of evil in the heavenly realms" (Ephesians 6:12). Suggestion: Place sign on or dangle it from the ceiling.

Sign 8: When Jesus returns, your battle with Satan is over, and you are the winner. "Thanks be to God! He gives us the victory through our Lord Jesus Christ" (1 Corinthians 15:57). Suggestion: Make paper clouds.

Sign 9: God has finished His work in you. You are free from the presence of Satan. No more temptation. No more sin. You are with God. Take an "I'm through with Satan" token. "God has given us eternal life, and this life is in his Son. He who has the Son has life; he who does not have the Son of God does not have life" (1 John 5:11, 12). Suggestion: String a line between two points. Place the "I'm through with Satan" tokens at this stop.

Step 2

Call the students to the large group area. "Today, we are learning reasons why it's cool to be a Christian. We know that a Christian is someone who has a personal relationship with Jesus. A Christian is someone who has salvation because of Jesus. When a person decides to have a relationship with

Jesus, he receives three things. The three things are listed in Philippians 1:6. Read the verse.

"Our small groups have put together nine stops to help us understand what these three things are." Before students begin walking through the stops, tell them where each stop is located, especially if it is outside the room. Tell students to take the stops in order from one to nine. Send students through the course in the manner you determine is best, one at a time, in pairs, or in small groups. Wait until one group is finished at a stop before allowing another group to begin.

When all students have returned from the nine stops, ask them to read the appropriate token in response to each of these statements.

Teacher: God began a good work in me when He forgave my sins.

Students: My penalty's paid.

Teacher: God continues His work in me by giving me a way out when I am tempted.

Students: I have power over sin.

Teacher: God will finish His work in me. When Jesus comes, I'll be free from Satan.

Students: I'm through with Satan.

Step 3

Before class, invite three adults to come to class and share how they celebrate their salvation. "Being a Christian is a reason to celebrate. The three gifts that we discovered are reasons to celebrate: the gift of salvation (forgiveness), help in daily living to resist temptation, and finally, freedom from the presence of Satan. Christians can celebrate because their sins have been forgiven. Jesus died in their place. Christians can celebrate because Jesus lives with them each day, helping them to stay away from sin. Christians can celebrate because they know that when Jesus returns, they will be finished with sin and Satan forever. Christians celebrate because of their salvation."

Have adult guests tell how they celebrate their salvation. Then share yourself.

"Early Christians celebrated their salvation too. One way they celebrated was in the way they greeted one another. Sometimes they would greet each other by using the word *Maranatha*. The word *Maranatha* means 'Come quickly Lord Jesus.'

"Another way early Christians celebrated their salvation was with a secret sign. It was the sign of a fish. The Greek word for fish is *ichthus* (ick-thoose). When the word fish is spelled in

Materials
three adults to share ways they celebrate their salvation

the Greek language, its letters form the first letters of each word in the phrase 'Jesus Christ, God's Son, Savior.'"

Take It to the Next Level

Materials
poster board or butcher paper, magazines, candy wrappers, comics, construction paper, newspaper, white glue, soft paint brushes

"We are going to celebrate salvation by making light switch plate covers. These switch plate covers will help us celebrate the work Jesus began in us when He forgave us of our sins. They will help us celebrate the fact that Jesus helps us live every day. They will help us celebrate our victory over Satan. They will help us celebrate salvation. We will put our switch plate covers in the church building where they will help other Christians celebrate too."

Students will make switch plate covers for classrooms in the church building. Provide at least one switch plate cover for each student. Secure permission from the necessary people before removing switch plates and decorating them. If it is not possible to decorate switch plate covers for the church building, provide covers that can be purchased at a discount store and have students make the covers for their rooms.

Provide magazines, candy wrappers, comics, newspapers, constructions paper, white glue, warm water, and soft paint brushes. Instruct pupils to cut out images to decorate their switch plate covers. Remind them not to cover the holes. Also remind them that these covers are to celebrate being a Christian. They might cut out letters and arrange the word *maranatha* on the cover. They might use pictures of fish. They might use the words *celebrate* or *salvation.*

When students are ready to glue their designs on the switch plate covers, mix three parts of white glue with one part warm water. Coat the back of each piece and then mount it on the switch plate cover. Apply a final layer of the glue when all pieces are in place. Set the plates aside to dry.

"These switch plates will greet many people as they walk into the classrooms in our church building.

"We have made them to help us celebrate being a Christian. They help us celebrate belonging to Jesus Christ. They help us celebrate our salvation. We learned some pretty cool things that Jesus does for those that belong to Him.

"Let's have a prayer time and thank God for the gifts that Jesus gives to Christians: forgiveness, help in our daily lives, and victory over Satan." Hand out the devotion cards for this week and encourage students to complete the activities suggested there.

Paying the Price

My penalty's paid.

NO FEAR

Cut out circles. Glue back to back.

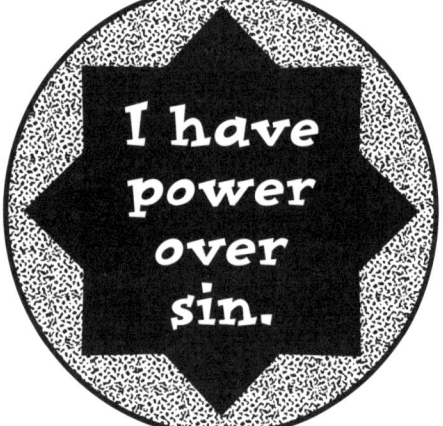

I have power over sin.

NO FEAR

Cut out circles. Glue back to back.

Copy one set of tokens for each student. Separate the strips and give the tokens to the appropriate group to prepare.

Cut out the front and back of each token. Glue them together.

I'm through with Satan.

NO FEAR

Cut out circles. Glue back to back.

110 ©1996 by The Standard Publishing Company. Permission is granted to reproduce this page for ministry purposes only—not for resale.

Session 4

Cool Stuff About the Church

Scripture. Hebrews 10:22-25; John 20:30, 31

Know that all Christians together are called the church.
Feel important to and needed by the church.
Describe each person's importance to the church.

Get Into the Game

Enlist four adults to present the skit "Spot the Impostors." Set the stage with three chairs, one for each guest. Provide a lectern for the host. Make a mask with a picture of your church building or another church building that will cover Guest #1's face. Provide some bricks or lumber for him or her to carry. No special dress requirements are needed for the host and Guests #2 and #3.

Materials
four adults, three chairs, lectern or podium, church building picture made into a mask, a few bricks or pieces of lumber, index cards, pencils, four photocopies of page 117

Step 1

"The Bible tells us more about what the church is like. It compares the church to three things—a body, a family, and a temple. We will work in small groups. Each group will examine one way the Bible describes the church." Explain the following activities. Then divide students into three groups, one group for each activity. Have an adult available to guide each group. "When our groups are finished, we will report back to everyone about what we learned."

Activity #1—A Body

Students will examine the comparison between the church and the body.

Roll out a long piece of butcher paper. Have a student lie down on the paper and trace around his or her body. Make two separate outlines. Tape the outlines to the wall.

"Each one of us has a body. We have just one body, but our bodies have many different parts. Each part is important because that part has a special job that only it can do." Enlist the help of the group to name and describe the jobs of five

Materials
butcher paper, markers, Bibles

body parts. For example: Eyes provide sight. Write each description on one of the body outlines in the appropriate place. "What would happen if every part of our bodies were eyes? ears? arms?" Discuss. Have students find and read 1 Corinthians 12:14-20.

"The writer of 1 Corinthians, Paul, tells us that the church is like a body. It has many different parts, yet it is still one body. The head of the church is Jesus." Write "Jesus is the head of the church" on the head of the second outline. "The parts of the church are people." Enlist the group to name five people in your local church and to describe the jobs they do. For example: Mrs. Davis orders Sunday school materials. Write each person and job on different places on the second body outline. Then read the following paraphrased version of 1 Corinthians 12:14-20 with the names and jobs that students listed.

"Now you are the body of Christ, and each one of you is a part of it. Now the church is not made up of one person but of many. If (name of first person) should say, 'Because I am not (name of second person), I do not belong to the church,' he (or she) would not for that reason cease to be part of the church. And if (name of third person) should say, 'Because I am not (name of fourth person), I do not belong to the church,' he (or she) would not for that reason cease to be a part of the church. If the whole church were (name of fourth person), who would do (job of first person)? If the whole church were (name of third person), who would do (job of second person)? But in fact God arranged the people in the church, every one of them just as He wanted them to be. If they all did the same job, where would the church be? As it is there are many people with different jobs, but only one church."

During the presentation, this group will show both body outlines. For the first outline, have a student read 1 Corinthians 12:14-20. For the second outline, have a student read the paraphrased version of 1 Corinthians 12:14-20.

Activity #2—A Family

Students will examine the comparison between the church and a family.

"Each one of us has a family. Our families are very different. One of us might have several brothers and sisters. One of us might be an only child. What is your family like?" Have students tell about their families. "Why is your family important?" Discuss. Help pupils conclude that family members love, support, and take care of one another.

"The Bible tells us that the church is a family. Who is the church's father?" Have pupils read Romans 8:14-16. "God is our father. Who are God's children?" Those who follow Jesus.

Materials
butcher paper or poster board, markers, Bibles, glue

"What does God's family do?" Have pupils read John 13:34. "God's children love one another.

"Since we are sons and daughters of God, we are brothers and sisters in God's family. Have you ever heard someone call a fellow Christian by the name brother or sister?" Call out the names of some of the students. Use brother in front of the boys' names and sister in front of the girls' names. For example: Brother Garrett and Sister Molly.

Have pupils make a collage. Take a section of butcher paper or poster board. Letter or have a student letter this title: We Are the Family of God.

Have students search through magazines and glue pictures of people of all ages to the poster.

When this group gives their presentation, have them walk through the audience and greet each person by using brother or sister before that person's first name. Then this group can show their poster and explain why the church is called the family of God.

Activity #3—A Temple

Students will examine the comparison between the church and a temple.

"Our church building is a beautiful building. Many people think that the building is the church. We learned from the skit that the church is people and not the building. The Bible does, however, compare the church to a building built with stone." Have students find and read Ephesians 2:19-22.

"Why is the foundation of a building important?" Discuss. (The foundation is the base upon which the building stands. It supports the building.) "Who is the foundation of the church?" (Apostles, prophets, Jesus.) "What is important about the cornerstone of a building?" (It is the first stone placed in the corner of the foundation. It holds the building together.) "Who is the cornerstone of the church?" (Jesus.) "Who are the stones in the church?" (Christians.)

Guide students to build a small structure out of the building blocks. The structure must have a foundation. Use masking tape and a marker to mark the blocks. Write Jesus on the cornerstone. Write some of the apostles names (Peter, James, John, Thomas, Philip, Matthew) on other blocks in the foundation. Write church members' names on blocks used to build the walls. Leave a section of the structure unbuilt. Have students write the names of class members on separate blocks and save them for their presentation.

During their presentation, this group will explain how they built their building, and how each part compares to the church. After explaining that Jesus forms the cornerstone and that the

Materials
building blocks, markers, masking tape, Bibles

apostles form the foundation, they should finish the structure by using the blocks with class members' names.

Step 2

Call students together. "Today we are learning about the church. We know that the church is people who follow and obey Jesus. Each one of our groups examined one way the Bible describes the church. They will help us understand more about the church.

"Group 1 examined why the church is called a body." Have Group 1 present their body outlines. "The church is called a body because it helps us understand that we need people with different talents and abilities. The church people work together using their different talents and abilities to spread the good news about Jesus.

"Group 2 examined why the church is called a family." Have Group 2 greet the class and present their poster. "The church is called a family because it help us understand how God loves us and how we should love others.

"Group 3 examined why the church is called a building." Have Group 3 show their building and finish adding the "class" blocks. "The church is called a building because it helps us understand that the each church member builds the kingdom of God on earth.

"These comparisons about the church help us understand what the church does and why the church is important. Christians need the help of others. We need the church as much as our bodies need our eyes and ears. We need the church as much as a family needs mom, dad, brother, and sister. We need the church as much as a building needs stones. We need the church and the church needs us."

Step 3

Before class, locate a puzzle with about fifty pieces. The puzzle must have all its pieces. Set aside one puzzle piece for each student. Put all of the remaining pieces together to start the puzzle.

"Each one of us is important and needed by the church. Most kids think that they are not very important to the church, but each one of you is important and the church needs you now. You don't have to wait until you are an adult to be needed by the church."

Distribute one puzzle piece to each student. Have students work together to put their pieces in the puzzle. "How is putting a puzzle together like being a part of the church?" Let students discuss.

Materials
simple puzzle, Bibles

"We all worked together to complete the puzzle. Each one of us had a piece that no one else had. Each piece was needed to complete the puzzle." Remove one piece to demonstrate. "Without this piece, the puzzle is not complete. Without you the church is not complete. It is missing someone. Each puzzle piece is not the same shape and does not fit in the same place, but each is equally important for completing the picture." Put puzzle piece back into puzzle. "We do not all serve in the same way, but we are all equally important and can help one another follow Jesus.

"Each one of us is important to the church. We're going to write statements that describe how important each one of us is to the church. We just used a puzzle to help us understand that we are important to the church. We could say, 'I'm as important to the church as each puzzle piece is to a puzzle.' Let's think of some more ways to show how important we are to the church." Some examples follow: I'm as important to the church as my eyes are to my body. I'm as important to the church as chocolate chips are to chocolate chip cookies. I'm as important to the church as a stone is to a building.

"We are important to the church, and the church needs us now to use our talents and abilities and to share what we have. We should not wait until we are adults to participate as important members of the church."

Have pupils find and read Hebrews 10:24, 25. "These verses tell us two important things that we can do right now to participate as important members of the church. What are they?" Discuss. "Verse 25 tells us to encourage one another by meeting together. One way that we take part in being the church is by gathering with other Christians. So when you attend worship, Sunday school, youth group, or Bible study, you are participating as an important part of the church.

"Verse 24 tells us to help one another show love by doing good deeds. Each of you can begin now to participate as important members of the church by using your talents and abilities. What can you do?" Discuss specifically what class members could do right now to participate as important members of the church. "Each one of us is important to the church because we can help one another live as God wants us to live." Have a student read John 20:30, 31. "We can encourage one another to believe that Jesus is the Son of God, and we can help one another have life in Jesus' name. Each one of us has a very important job in the church."

Take It to the Next Level

Materials
puzzle pieces from an incomplete puzzle, white acrylic paint, paint brush, safety pins, fabric tape, fine-point permanent markers, pencils

Before class, gather puzzle pieces from incomplete puzzles. Large pieces are preferred. Paint each piece with white acrylic paint and allow pieces to dry. During class, give each student one puzzle piece. Students should use a fine-point permanent marker to write on the puzzle pieces. Instruct students to use a pencil to plan for placement and size of words before using the permanent marker. Instruct pupils to write "I'm an important piece" on the puzzle pieces. Attach a safety pin to the back of each puzzle piece with a piece of fabric tape. As students work, discuss with them what they can say when people ask them to explain their puzzle pieces.

Optional: Have students make enough puzzle piece pins to distribute to church members. Designate a Sunday morning when students can distribute the puzzle pins and explain their meaning.

When students have completed the puzzle pieces, have them gather in a circle. Read John 20:30, 31 again. "The purpose of the church is to carry the message about Jesus so that many people can believe and have life in Jesus' name. Each one of us is important to the church because each of us can carry the message about Jesus."

Close with prayer. Distribute this week's devotional cards and encourage students to study it each day.

Spot the Impostors

Host: Hi! I'm Debbie (Danny) Daniels. Welcome to Spot the Impostors. Today, we have three very interesting guests. Only one of our guests is who he claims to be. Let's meet them.

(Guests enter one at a time, introduce themselves, and take a seat)

Guest #1: Hello, I'm the church.

Guest #2: Howdy, I'm the church.

Guest #3: Hi, I'm the church.

Host: Each one of our guests claims to be the church. Audience, it is your job to decide which one of these guests is the real church. Let's begin. Church guests, please tell us where you live.

Guest #1: I'm located at the corner of Carson and Cody Streets.

Guest #2: I live at 7116 Northridge Drive, Apartment #2.

Guest #3: I live on a farm, six miles from the city.

Host: What is your job?

Guest #1: I'm a building. I shelter people while they learn about Jesus.

Guest #2: I work for the telephone company.

Guest #3: I tell people about Jesus.

Host: Why are you called the church?

Guest #1: When people say, "Let's go to church," they are talking about me. Everyone I know calls me the church.

Guest #2: I go to church. Everyone who goes to church is the church.

Guest #3: My name is Tracy. I am the church because I follow and obey Jesus.

Host: What is the church?

Guest #1: It's a place where people meet to worship God and study the Bible.

Guest #2: It's people who go to church.

Guest #3: It's people who follow and obey Jesus.

Host: Audience, it's time to vote. Which one of these three guests is the church? Mark your card with #1, #2, or #3. Vote for the guest whom you believe is the real church.

(Distribute index cards and pencils. Have students mark the cards with their choice. Pick up and count the votes.)

Host: Who does the audience believe is the real church? *(Reveal vote tally.)* Is the audience right or wrong? Will the real church please stand up? *(Guest #3 stands.)* Guest #3 is the real church. Tell us again why you are the church.

Guest #3: Debbie, the church is everyone who follows and obeys Jesus. The church is people. It is not a building. It is not just anyone who visits a church building on Sunday. The church is all people everywhere who follow and obey Jesus.

Host: I want to thank all three of our guests for being here on the show today. We have a special gift for each one. Thanks to our audience. We'll see you next time on "Spot the Impostors."

117   ©1996 by The Standard Publishing Company. Permission is granted to reproduce this page for ministry purposes only—not for resale.

Bridge the Gap

Cool Stuff About Bible Times

Understanding the manners and customs of Bible times is essential when wanting to understand the Bible. The Jewish culture was very different from western culture. This session is intended to introduce your students to a few of the common manners and customs of Bible days.

Use a large room or area in your church building or use several rooms that are grouped together. Set up carnival-type booths to demonstrate customs and manners of Bible times. Each fair attendee should be given three paper denarii at the entrance to the fair. Photocopy one set of coins (three denarii and one didrachma) from page 124 for each person who attends the fair. During the course of the fair, students will be told what to do with the paper coins.

Recruit some of the students' parents and older siblings to conduct the activities of the booths. Volunteers should dress in Bible-times clothing and be prepared to discuss and explain the manner or custom of that booth. Give the workers the following information for their respective booths. The information offered here is limited, but your fair doesn't have to be limited to these ideas alone. Books on manners and customs of Bible times will give you ideas and insights for additional booths.

Materials
photocopies of coins from page 124, scissors

Booth #1. Clothing

For this booth, ask a man and woman to dress in traditional Bible-times clothing. They will talk with guests about Bible-times clothing and provide various pieces for students to try on. These volunteers should gather their clothing based on these descriptions and drawings.

Tunic. The basic piece of clothing was something like a sack. A V-shaped opening was cut for the head, and slits were made in the corners for the arms. Until the time of Jesus, the tunic was made of two pieces of fabric sewn together around the center. Looms able to weave the tunic in one piece were invented in Jesus' day. Jesus' tunic was woven in one piece (John 19:23).

Men's tunics were normally short, about knee length. Women's tunics were ankle-length. People in Bible times wore the tunic as nightclothes.

Girdle. The tunic was held to the waist by a long, wide piece of fabric called a girdle. Today, we would call it a belt. The person wearing the girdle would hold one end of the folded fabric to his waist and give the other end to a friend to hold. The person putting on the girdle would turn around and around until he got to the end of the fabric. He tucked the end in to hold everything together. Some girdles were made of leather and held together with clasps.

When men needed freedom of movement, they pulled up the hem of the tunic and tucked it into the girdle. This was called girding up your loins. When a Bible writer used

the phrase "gird up your loins," he meant to be ready for action. The girdle was used to hold money, tools, or weapons.

Cloak or Mantle. The cloak was a large square of cloth with armholes. It was worn over the tunic. It usually fell to or below the knees. It was used

much like overcoats are used today. It was also used as a blanket at night. Most people in Bible times only had one cloak. It was a person's most valuable possession. A piece of clothing was a valuable gift.

The cloak was used to carry things. It was often filled with grain or fruit. A person could even carry a small lamb in the "lap" of his cloak. The law required men to wear tassels at the corners of the cloak or mantle. One thread of each tassel was to be blue as a reminder to obey the commandments of God (Numbers 15:38, 39). Women decorated their clothing with embroidery, strings of coins, or other ornaments. Men and women were forbidden by God's law to wear each other's clothing (Deuteronomy 22:5).

Headwear. Often a square of cloth was draped over the head and held in place by a headband. Some men wrapped the cloth to give the appearance of a turban. Women wore a square of material that was folded to make a sunshield for the eyes. It fell over the shoulders and was held in place by a braided cord. The head scarf was also used as a veil to cover the face. Headwear provided valuable protection from the sun and weather.

Sandals. People of Bible times wore sandals. The sole was made of wood or leather and fastened to the foot with leather straps. Walking on dusty roads in sandals made the people's feet very dirty. It was customary to remove their sandals and receive a foot bath when they entered someone's house.

Booth #2. Welcoming Guests

Set up an area to demonstrate how guests were welcomed into a Bible-times home. The area should give the feel of a home. A canopy tent with open sides would work well for this. Supply the area with throw rugs, large pillows, and chairs. Provide a tub large enough for feet (preferably ceramic), water to pour over the feet (in a ceramic pitcher), towels, olive oil in a small ceramic container with lid, drinking water in a ceramic pitcher, and paper cups.

Welcome students in Bible-lands style. This ritual included a greeting, removing the shoes, washing the feet, anointing the head with oil, and giving the guest a drink of water. Explain the welcome as students participate.

Greetings. Guests in Bible-time homes expected to be greeted with a kiss. The most formal form of a kiss greeting involved placing hands on each other's shoulders then pulling together and giving a kiss on the right cheek and then on the left. The most honored guests were greeted with a bow which was either a movement of the head forward or a bending at the waist. Verbal forms of greeting included the words, "Rejoice," "Greetings," or "Peace be with you." Some greetings included all three of these things. First, the host bowed to the guest. Next, he spoke words of greeting. Finally, he kissed the guest.

Removing the Shoes/Foot Washing. Use a tub or bowl large enough for feet, a pitcher for pouring water, water, and towels. Have the guest sit in a chair. Perform the foot washing by removing the shoes, pouring water over the guest's feet, rubbing them with your hands, and drying them with the towel. While washing the feet of the guests, explain the custom.

Anytime this booth runs out of water, tell the guest that you must go to the well for more water. Use a large pitcher, preferably ceramic. Carry the pitcher on your head.

Guests always removed their shoes before entering a home. This was so that they would not carry any dirt into the house. In addition, they could sit with their feet beneath them and not soil the couch or their clothing. Shoes were also removed for foot washing.

Washing dirty feet was a common courtesy in Bible times. Wearing sandals when walking on dusty roads caused people's feet to get very dirty. When a guest arrived at a home in Bible times, his or her feet would probably be washed by a servant of the house. The task of foot washing was considered a humble task to be performed by servants. When Jesus washed the feet of His disciples at the last supper, He was teaching them to be servants of God's people.

Anointing the Head With Oil. Provide olive oil or vegetable oil in a small ceramic container with a lid.

After the foot washing, anoint the guests' heads with oil by dipping a finger in the oil and rubbing it across the forehead.

Olive oil mixed with spices was used to anoint the head. Anointing the head was a sign of honor and welcome.

Giving a Drink of Water. Pour each guest a drink of water.

The giving of a drink of water was significant because it was a pledge of friendship. It showed that the guest had received a peaceful welcome into the host's home. Jesus said, "Anyone who gives you a cup of water in my name because you belong to Christ will certainly not lose his reward."

Women drew water from a nearby well. They carried the heavy jars filled with water on their heads. They usually drew water in the morning or evening.

Booth #3. Money

Set up two tables. Gather some "Bible-times" containers such as small ceramic pots and drawstring bags. These will be used to hold the paper "coins." Photocopy the Bible-times coins (page 124). Cut them out. Place the didrachma coins in the container at the money changer's table. Make sure each guest receives three denarii when entering the fair area.

Temple Tax. One member of this booth should be a roving temple tax collector. He should walk around the fair asking students to pay the temple tax. When students enter the fair area, they will be given three paper denarii. They will use two of the denarii to exchange for a two-drachma (didrachma) coin, which is the correct temple tax currency. When students try to pay the tax with the denarii, the collector will direct them to the money changer to exchange the money. After the money is exchanged, students may return to the tax collector to pay the temple tax. This volunteer should write down each name as the tax is paid so that he will not miss asking anyone for the tax.

Jesus paid the temple tax, but He did not go to the money changers to get the coin He needed. Instead, He told Peter to fish for the money. Jesus told Peter he would find a four-drachma coin in the mouth of the first fish he caught. Peter did, and he paid his and Jesus' temple tax (Matthew 17:24-27).

Money Changers. The temple tax collector will send students to this table to exchange two denarii for a two-drachma (didrachma) coin (two denarii = two drachma) to pay the temple tax. This person should have an abundant supply of paper two-drachma coins.

Money changers were the bankers of Jesus' day. They exchanged money, took deposits, and made loans. They charged interest for the loans they made. Charging interest was against God's laws. Money changers set up their tables in the temple. Jesus drove them out. They did not belong in God's house. The temple was a place of prayer, not a place to cheat people (Matthew 21:13).

In Jesus' day, coins from other countries were used in Palestine. Only one kind of currency—the Greek drachma—was accepted to pay the temple tax of two drachma. People who did not have this currency were forced to exchange their money for the kind of money accepted for the tax. They did this at the table of the money changer where they were charged to exchange their money.

Tax Collectors. The person sitting at this table will tax "goods" that enter the fair. He should stop those who pass by and examine the items they are carrying and charge each a tax of one denarii.

In Jesus' day, Bible lands were ruled by the Roman government. The Jews had to pay taxes to the Romans. Roman tax contractors hired local Jewish people to collect taxes for the Roman government. Tax collectors were not liked because they worked for Rome and because they charged more tax than what was due. Tax collectors were considered among the worst sinners because they had regular contact with foreigners.

Jesus cared for tax collectors. He visited the home of Zaccheus who was a chief tax collector, one who hired tax collectors for the Roman government. See Luke 19:2-10. Jesus called Matthew to follow Him and even ate dinner with Matthew and some of his tax collector friends. See Matthew 9:9-11.

Taxes were collected on land, personal property, individuals, and goods coming into the country or city. Matthew was at his tax collector's booth when Jesus called him. Matthew was probably collecting tax on goods brought into the city.

Booth #4. Light

Gather several oil-burning lamps and lamp oil. Set up one area to display the burning lamps and another where students can make simple clay lamps. Display pictures of Bible-times lamps or the drawing provided with this lesson. Provide self-hardening clay, dull knives, rolling pins, scissors, wax paper, and the patterns from page 124. Provide these instructions for making a lamp similar to a Bible-times lamp.

1. Knead the clay until it is soft and easy to mold.

2. Use the rolling pin to roll out the clay on wax paper. Flatten the clay to about ¼-inch thick.

3. Lay the patterns over the clay and use the dull knife to cut them out.

4. Lay the lamp piece with holes on top of the piece without holes.

5. Mold the pieces together to form a lamp.

6. Allow the clay to dry.

While students are working on their lamps, guide the conversation with the following information.

In Bible lands, night was a time of danger from robbers and unfriendly neighbors. People were afraid of the dark. There was no electricity, no street lights or porch lights. People of Jesus' day used oil lamps for light. Lamps burned all night in Jewish homes. A dark house meant the family was extremely poor or that the house was deserted.

Lamps were made of clay. A wick made of flax burned olive oil. Lamps had two holes, one for the wick and one to pour in the oil. Lamps were placed in small openings in the walls, on a lamp stand, or on a bushel. A bushel in Bible days was a bowl that held about eight quarts of dry grain like wheat.

Light was valuable to the people of Jesus' day. They did not hide their lamps. Instead, they put their lamps where they would give light to everyone in the house. Jesus told His followers that they are like light. They are as important to the world as a light is to a dark room. See Matthew 5:15, 16.

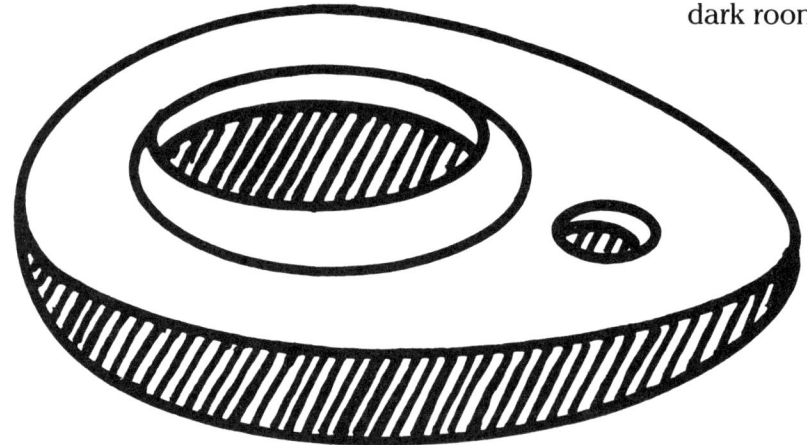

Booth #5. Food

Set up a snack bar with the following common Bible-times foods: bread, olives, grapes, almonds, pistachio nuts, citrus fruit, cheese, and yogurt. If possible, make homemade bread so that students can break off pieces of it to eat.

Bread was the staple of the Jewish diet. It was so basic and so important in Jesus' day that Jesus called himself the "bread of life." See John 6:35.

Bread was always broken, not cut with a knife, which is why Bible writers use the phrase "to break bread." This phrase refers to eating a meal together. It also refers to the Lord's Supper. See Acts 2:42-47; 20:7.

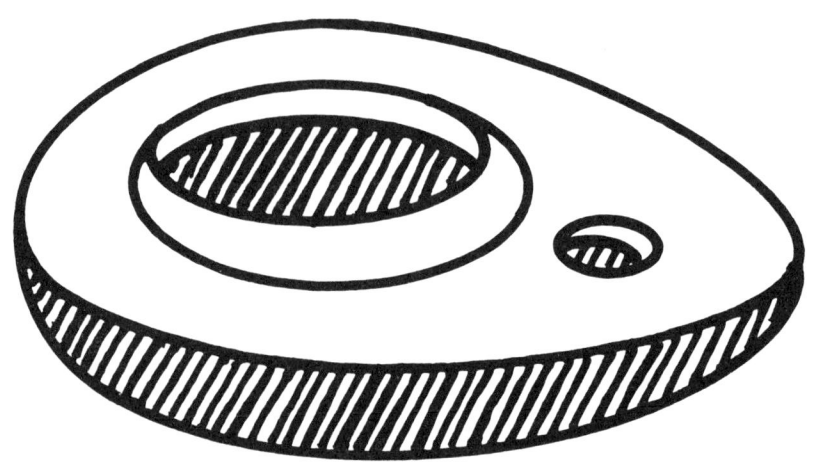

Bible Lamp
(Booth #4)

Bible Money
(Booth #3)

 ©1996 by The Standard Publishing Company. Permission is granted to reproduce this page for ministry purposes only—not for resale.

Newcomer Packets

Welcome to Our Way Cool Church

Students will make newcomer packets for children in grades 1-6. This project will serve as a review for this unit of lessons. It will also acquaint students with church staff and church programs.

Packet Jacket

Decide the number of newcomer packets your group wants to make. Make one copy of pages 127 and 128 for each packet. Make a sample copy of the jacket so that students will have a reference copy.

Because of the nature of photocopies, art work and folding and cutting lines are included together on the reproducible. Cutting lines will not show because they will be cut away. Fold lines will show. However, once you study the placement of the packet folds, you will not need the fold lines. They can be covered with correction fluid before copying so they will not show on the finished jacket.

Packet Cards

Students will make seven cards for the packet. (An optional card called "Kids in the Bible" can be photocopied from page 128 for the packet.)

For each packet cut paper 3 ½ inches wide for the cards.

Make two cards 5 ¾ inches high.

Make two cards 5 inches high.

Make two cards 4 ¼ inches high.

Make one card 3 ½ inches high. If you are using the "Kids in the Bible" card, make two cards this size.

Use the titles given on page 128. Glue them onto the cards you have prepared.

Students may want to decorate the cards.

Place the following cards in the left pocket of the jacket: Cool Stuff About the Bible (5 ¾"), Cool Stuff About Jesus (5"), Cool Stuff About Christians (4 ¼"), and Cool Stuff About the Church (3 ½"). Place the following cards in the right pocket of the jacket: Cool People (5 ¾"), Cool Places to Be (5"), Way Cool Fun (4 ¼"), Kids in the Bible (3 ½").

Gather Information for the Cards

Work together as a group to determine the information for the four cards that will summarize the lessons from this unit. Students can tell what they learned about each topic. List their statements on the chalkboard. Then choose which ones to include on that topic card. This information can be included on the card in a list format. For example:

The Bible
—Is God's Word
—Was written by 40 men over 1500 years
—Has 66 books
—Tells God's message of salvation

Use this method to make a card for the Bible, Jesus, Christians, and the Church.

For the remaining cards, invite the minister, church leader, or children's department leader to tell the students about the church staff, other teachers in the children's department, the regular church schedule, and special events for kids. List these as they are mentioned. Then decide what to include.

Decide how you will transfer the information to the cards. Students can write the information or a volunteer can type the information. Whatever method you choose, check for accuracy, spelling, and punctuation.

When the cards are completed, arrange them to photocopy. Make sure each card is outlined because the cards will need to be cut apart after they are photocopied.

If your church has a pamphlet for kids about salvation or about joining your congregation, include one in the packet.

Be sure to make several copies of the packet to keep on hand for future use.

Jacket Instructions

1. Cut out the jacket following the solid lines.
2. Fold on the dashed lines. Fold side tabs to the inside.
   Fold bottom flaps to the inside. Fold in half.
3. Glue tabs to the inside to form a pocket.

glue here

Welcome to Our

Way Cool

Church

"Jesus did many other miraculous signs in the presence of his disciples, which are not recorded in this book. But these are written that you may believe that Jesus is the Christ, the Son of God, and that by believing, you may

have life in his name" (John 20:30, 31, *NIV*). Jesus loves kids! Read more verses to learn how much Jesus loves kids: Psalm 127:3; Mark 10:13-16.

Sayings From the Bible

Have you ever wondered where these sayings came from?

They came from the Bible. Go ahead, look them up. Use a *King James Version* Bible.

- The Handwriting on the Wall (Daniel 5)

- Spare the Rod and Spoil the Child (Proverbs 13:24)

- The Powers that Be (Romans 13:1)

- The Skin of Your Teeth (Job 19:20)

- A Wolf in Sheep's Clothing (Matthew 7:15-20)

- The Apple of My Eye (Deuteronomy 32:10)

- An Eye for an Eye (Exodus 21:24)

- A Drop in the Bucket (Isaiah 40:15)

glue here

127 ©1996 by The Standard Publishing Company. Permission is granted to reproduce this page for ministry purposes only—not for resale.

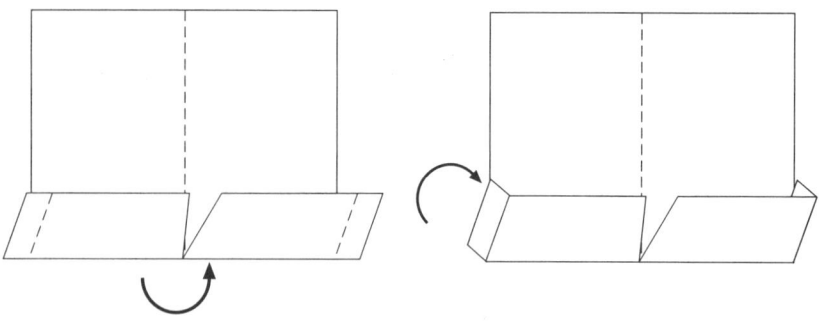

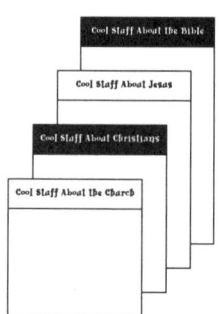

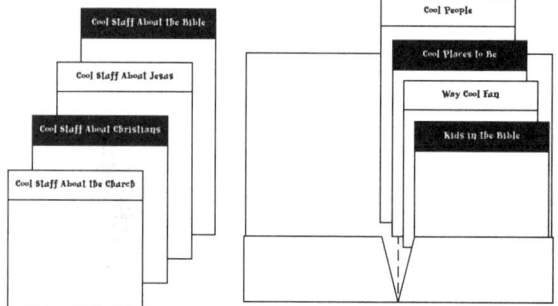

Cool Stuff About the Bible

Cool Stuff About Jesus

Cool Stuff About Christians

Cool Stuff About the Church

Newcomer Packet Inserts

Cool People

Cool Places to Be

Way Cool Fun

Kids in the Bible

Kids in the Bible

1. What three kids became kings of Judah? How old were they? Read 2 Kings 11:21; 21:1; 22:1.
2. What child took his first trip in a basket? Read Exodus 2:1-10.
3. Who hid when he was about to be chosen king? Read 1 Samuel 10:17-27.
4. What kid taught the teachers of the Law at the Temple? Read Luke 2:41-47.
5. What kid did God wake up in the middle of the night? Read 1 Samuel 3:1-19.
6. Who was the best dressed kid in the Bible? Read Genesis 37:3.

 ©1996 by The Standard Publishing Company. Permission is granted to reproduce this page for ministry purposes only—not for resale.